THE COLLECTED POEMS
OF WELDON KEES

(Third Edition)

Edited by Donald Justice

Introduction to the new Bison Books
Edition by David Wojahn

UNIVERSITY OF NEBRASKA PRESS • LINCOLN

Introduction © 2003 by the University of Nebraska Press
© 1975, 1962 by the University of Nebraska Press
© 1960 by John A. Kees
© 1954, 1947, 1943 by Weldon Kees
Manufactured in the United States of America

∞

First Nebraska paperback printing: 1962

Library of Congress Cataloging-in-Publication Data
Kees, Weldon, b. 1914.
The collected poems of Weldon Kees / edited by Donald Justice;
introduction to the Bison Books edition by David Wojahn.—3rd ed.
p.   cm.
ISBN 0-8032-7809-8 (pbk.: alk. paper)
I. Justice, Donald Rodney, 1925–   II. Title.
PS3521.E285A17   2003
811'.52—dc21
2003051362

INTRODUCTION

David Wojahn

When the first edition of *The Collected Poems of Weldon Kees* was published in 1960, Weldon Kees was an all-but-forgotten figure. Although his poems had appeared in some of the most prominent journals of the 1940s and 1950s and he had published three collections of verse, instead of being remembered for his poetry Kees was probably better remembered for his membership in that sadly large group of literary suicides—in the summer of 1955 his car was found abandoned on the approach to San Francisco's Golden Gate Bridge, from which he had probably jumped. The Stone Wall Press collection of all of Kees's poems seemed to hold little hope of changing the poet's status. The volume appeared in a fine press edition of only two hundred copies, and the poems gathered there had little in common with what came to be the prevailing poetic concerns of the coming decade. Kees's poetry exhibited nothing Surrealist, Beat, or Confessional, and in an era during which verse in open forms became the prosodic party line Kees's frequent reliance on received forms and meters made his writing look decidedly out of date. Kees's stance also had to be considered: in his introduction to the volume, editor Donald Justice characterized Kees as "one of the bitterest poets in history." The odds against Kees receiving any sort of posthumous recognition were very high indeed. Nevertheless, in his introduction Justice asserted that Kees was "an important poet, one of the three or four best of his generation." It was a bold claim, given the fact that Kees belonged to a literary generation whose members included Robert Lowell, Elizabeth Bishop, John Berryman, Randall Jarrell, Muriel Rukeyser, George Oppen, and Theodore Roethke.

In the forty-three years since this book's original publication Kees's reputation has steadily grown. Justice's once-brash claim for Kees's significance is now shared by a good many readers, critics, and poets. Kees, who once seemed destined for literary oblivion, has been championed by critics on both sides of the Atlantic; his work has appeared in a number of anthologies of twentieth-century American verse and he has been the subject of a substantial biography by James Reidel (Nebraska, 2003). An edition of Kees's letters, a collection of his short stories, and a volume of his reviews and essays have been published as well. Most important, his work has influenced several generations of American poets, many of whom were not yet born when Kees took his plunge from the bridge. Thanks to the University of Nebraska Press, which first reprinted Kees's *Collected Poems* in 1962, his verse has remained in print for most of the past four decades. Despite the bitterness and rejection that Kees knew during his lifetime, his afterlife is a literary success story.

Weldon Kees was born in Beatrice, Nebraska, in 1914, the son of a successful merchant. While attending Doane College and the University of Nebraska he began to publish stories and poems in the small magazines of the day. He later began work on a novel, *Fall Quarter*, which remained unpublished until 1990. From the time of his graduation from college until his death Kees made his living mainly as a librarian and as a professional writer, working first for the Federal Writers' Project and, for a time during the 1940s, as a movie reviewer for *Time Magazine*. Kees never stayed put for long, living variously in Denver, New York City, Provincetown, Massachusetts, and finally San Francisco. His restlessness suggests something of Kees's near-manic energy: he carried on an extensive correspondence with many of the best-known literary figures of his day, he exhibited his paintings with the abstract expressionists, he wrote songs and screenplays, he played in traditional jazz bands, and he coauthored a study of nonverbal communication illustrated with his own quite striking photographs. James Reidel's biography of Kees paints a picture of a character who could have stepped out of hard-boiled fiction or film noir of the time, a restless, agitated soul always on the lookout for the Big Score—which invariably eludes him. The reasons for Kees's apparent suicide aren't entirely clear, but whatever vitality Kees displays in his letters and in his relentless literary and artistic activity belies the grimly dyspeptic worldview of his poems. In the decades since Donald Justice first called Kees one of the bitterest poets in history the world has seen figures who are arguably far more bitter (Philip Larkin comes to mind). But no one is bitter in quite the same way as Weldon Kees was bitter; he was a remarkably resourceful and inventive poet and his manner was unmistakably his own.

Like Elizabeth Bishop, Kees hit upon his mature voice early, and his debut collection, *The Last Man* (published in 1943), contains some of his most characteristic poems, notably "The Smiles of the Bathers," "After the Trial," and "For My Daughter." The latter poem stands with Robert Frost's "Design" as one of the bleakest sonnets in the language. The nihilism and sense of cultural exhaustion displayed in it and in other poems in the volume derive in part from T. S. Eliot and W. H. Auden, the most influential poets of Kees's day. But the theme of spiritual crisis and the drive for spiritual renewal found in their work is entirely absent in Kees's. His are poems in which, as Kafka put it, "the dreadful has already happened" and the apocalypse has run its course. Kees's speakers are left to navigate the world's ruins, and for self-protection they possess nothing but their doggedness and mordant wit. In this respect Kees less resembles his modernist peers than postmodernist figures such as the playwright Samuel Beckett.

The character of Robinson, Kees's alter ego and the subject of four of his later poems, is a kind of cold war–era everyman. In his "glen plaid jacket, Scotch grain shoes . . . , / Black four in hand and oxford button down," Robinson epitomizes the conformity of the 1950s—and also the decade's inherent sense of dread. His is a ghostly, alienated presence with a "sad and usual heart, dry as a winter leaf." Other of Kees's creations are even more unsettling. In "The Testimony of James Apthorp" Kees enters the mind of a psychotic killer. The speaker of "The Clinic" comes to see the madhouse as a microcosm of existence, writing at the poem's conclusion that "we came into that room / Where a world of cats danced, spat and howled / Upon a burning plate.—And I was home." Kees is not a poet for the faint of heart.

What saves such poems from redundancy and gratuitousness is Kees's unassuming mastery of technique. "The whole style of his poetry," says Donald Justice, "lies in its very unobtrusiveness." Kees's language is unadorned yet his command of form is considerable. It amounts to what Justice, whose own poetry owes a significant debt to Kees, calls Kees's "apparently artless setting down of the facts. Without trickery, and in the right order." Like Elizabeth Bishop, Kees has a way of making difficult reckonings and complicated poetic forms—such as the sestina and the villanelle—look effortless. Yet he is never glib and never interested in the easy tour de force; he favors the villanelle and the sestina in part because their refrains and repetitions replicate the circular and obsessive nature of his themes. And, whether he was working in received forms or in free verse, few poets employed repetition as devastatingly as Kees. Take, for example, "1926," which I quote in its entirety:

The porchlight coming on again,
Early November, the dead leaves
Raked in piles, the wicker swing
Creaking. Across the lots
A phonograph is playing *Ja-Da*.

An orange moon. I see the lives
Of neighbors, mapped and marred

Like all the wars ahead, and R.
Insane, B., with his throat cut,
Fifteen years from now, in Omaha.

I did not know them then.
My airedale scratches at the door
And I am back from seeing Milton Sills
And Doris Kenyon. Twelve years old.
The porchlight coming on again.

Milton Sills and Doris Kenyon were film stars of the silent era, forgotten figures today. It is gratifying to know that such a fate seems to have escaped Weldon Kees. With this third edition of *Collected Poems* a new generation of readers can encounter Kees's eerie and indelible voice. The politics of literary reputation are of course mysterious; poets touted as major figures at one time or another are often later relegated to oblivion. Is Weldon Kees a major poet? He is surely a significant one, and it seems that the quiet, sustained ferocity of his poetry has won readers more loyal than those supposedly claimed by many major poets. We have every reason to expect that such will continue to be the case.

PREFACE TO THE REVISED EDITION

Fifteen years have passed since this collection was hand-set by two young printers, Raeburn Miller and K. K. Merker, in an edition of two hundred copies. Poets as well as printers, they had come to share my admiration for the poems here collected, as others have since come to do, thanks to the subsequent paperback edition which made the poems more readily available.

Out of print for several years, this paperback edition has now been slightly revised. To it the poet's father had added, at the end of the section of "Uncollected Poems," six pieces from among his son's literary remains. Four of these represented early work, published in periodicals or anthologies during the Second World War and not thereafter reprinted by the poet himself; they are therefore omitted from the present collection. A fifth of that group is to be found here as the last part of "Speeches and Lyric for a Play," where the poet had placed it. The sixth poem, "To Build a Quiet City in His Mind," I have felt should be retained, on its merits. I have placed it first in the final section, however, in accord with my desire to arrange the poems in approximate chronological order, so far as I could estimate it, an intention declared in the original preface but, owing to circumstances not in my control, never till now carried out. One poem, "First Anniversary," has been added to this section.

No doubt other fugitive pieces exist, some unknown to me, as well as manuscript copies I have not seen. The reasons, however, for not attempting a critical edition remain as obvious to me as they did fifteen years ago. Should the demand ever arise, it would please me if someone were to devote the right care to such an edition. I would be especially pleased if such an editor had known the poet, as I did not. The reasons for undertaking what I saw as my own more limited task will, I hope, be obvious as well. I liked the poems and I thought they should be made available by whatever means lay to hand. As far as I know, no one else had, in 1960, felt quite that way.

DONALD JUSTICE

PREFACE

Of the three volumes of poetry published by Weldon Kees not one is at present easily obtainable. There is little mention of him in the histories of twentieth-century American poetry; he is not represented in the current anthologies. It is possible that his poems are no longer read; probably they were never very widely read; and yet it seems to me that he is an important poet, among the three or four best of his generation.

Weldon Kees was born February 24, 1914, at Beatrice, Nebraska. By the time of his graduation from the University of Nebraska in 1935, he was publishing fiction in literary magazines of the Middle West. Two years later his first published poem, "Subtitle," appeared in an obscure little magazine called *Signatures*. From that time on he was chiefly a poet.

Leaving an editorial job with the Federal Writers' Project in Lincoln, he moved to Denver in 1937, where eventually he became director of the Bibliographical Center of Research for the Rocky Mountain Region. By 1943 he was in New York, writing for *Time* and helping make documentary films. There also, in the mid-forties, he began to paint. His paintings were exhibited in one-man shows at the Peridot Gallery and on at least one occasion were shown along with paintings by Hans Hofmann, de Kooning, and others of the abstract expressionist movement, with which his work in this field can be associated. In 1951 he left New York in its turn for San Francisco.

On the West Coast he took up jazz piano with some seriousness and began to compose, jazz tunes mostly, but also the score to an experimental film, "The Adventures of Jimmy."

He himself made a few movies. He collaborated with Dr. Jurgen Ruesch, a University of California psychiatrist, on a book called *Non-Verbal Communication,* which is illustrated with hundreds of stunning photographs, also by Kees.

Meanwhile he found time to paint and to write the poems which make up his last book. Up to this point his career, aside from its astonishing versatility, remains a fairly typical career for any writer reaching manhood in the depression and passing through a time of political crisis and war.

It was on July 18, 1955, that *The New Republic* printed a review by Kees entitled "How to Be Happy: Installment 1053," in which the following passage appears: "In our present atmosphere of distrust, violence, and irrationality, with so many human beings murdering themselves—either literally or symbolically. . . ." On that day his car was found abandoned on the approach to the Golden Gate Bridge. He had spoken to friends of suicide; he had also spoken of going away to start a new life, perhaps in Mexico. Scattered throughout his poems are lines which, as we read them now, seem to foreshadow this final event, whatever it may have been. If the whole of his poetry can be read as a denial of the values of the present civilization, as I believe it can, then the disappearance of Kees becomes as symbolic an act as Rimbaud's flight or Crane's suicide.

The poetry of Kees makes its deepest impression when read as a body of work rather than a collection of isolated moments of brilliance. This may account in part for the neglect from which it has suffered. Though a number of the poems are brilliant and many are moving, no single poem perhaps is flawless. There are no epics, no dramas, none of those long ambitious poems on which the most conspicuous contemporary reputations are founded. Moreover, the taste at work is throughout of a kind which forbids the glittering surfaces of a more fashionable poetry. But there is a cumulative power to the work as a whole to which even the weaker poems contribute.

Kees is original in one of the few ways that matter: he speaks to us in a voice or, rather, in a particular tone of voice which we have never heard before. In the early poems, it is true, there are echoes of other poets. But almost immediately he found his proper tone. Already in his first book it can be heard in such a poem as "For My Daughter," with the terrible but quiet shock of its last line. And almost always his is a quiet voice. That will not seem very surprising until one pauses to consider how very bitter are the things this quiet voice has to say.

For Kees is one of the bitterest poets in history. "Others," wrote Kenneth Rexroth, "have called themselves Apocalyptics, Kees lived in a permanent and hopeless apocalypse." Yet he appears to accept whatever is, however terrifying or ridiculous it may seem, with the serenity of a saint. The wall cracks; the stain spreads; he does not budge from his chair. This calm in the face of a certain doom, the most characteristic attitude of his poetry, is the ultimate expression of the bitterness at the center of his work; it is also a curious anticipation of the atomic despair so familiar now, though arrived at by Kees some years before the bomb.

The bitterness may be traced to a profound hatred for a botched civilization, Whitman's America come to a dead end on the shores of the Pacific. On the last three decades of American culture, and especially on whatever is pretentious or phony, Kees turns the eye of a satirist. His eye for the satiric detail is one of his most remarkable talents, and the texture of many poems whose purpose is not satiric depends on this special type of Keesian ornament. The merely satiric poems, however, seem to me not his best. His satire is best when it is mixed, when the scorn is mingled with pity, as in the series concerning Robinson, his typical man.

To originality in style and technique his poetry would seem to lay little claim. Yet since the whole style of his poetry lies in its very unobtrusiveness, it is a crucial part of his individual tone. It is a style which answers to what seems to me the classical definition of a good *prose* style: natural words in a natural order. His work in fact, belongs to what might be called the Prose Tradition in poetry.

This is not to say that Kees ignores the technical matters which are the major concern of another type of poet. Many of his poems are formal. He toys with the villanelle and that elaborate form the sestina. So far as I know, "After the Trial" is the first truly prosy sestina, though Kipling had tried the form in Cockney. With the devices of enumeration, repetition, and variation, which have attracted so many modern poets, Kees experiments endlessly, from the early "Fugue" to the late "Round." The traditional meters, when he chooses to employ them, are treated with a good deal of freedom, in obedience to the law of naturalness which guides his ear. The result is that the verse of many poems, especially the later ones, is neither quite metered nor quiet free. In some of these his technique has been reduced to its essence, which is nothing more than the apparently artless setting down of the facts, without trickery, and in the right order. In the process, in such a poem as "1926," prose may be said to have become lyric.

The aim of the present collection is to make his poetry once more available, and available in a form complete enough to provide the basis for an appreciation of his work as a whole. It is hoped that a larger edition may follow the present limited one. For obvious reasons, no critical edition has been attempted; nor are these the complete poems, for a few fugitive poems in magazines have been excluded. However, *The Last Man, The Fall of the Magicians,* and *Poems: 1947–1954,* which contain all the poems written up to some time in 1954 that Kees apparently thought complete or wished to preserve, are included entire. Part Four of his second book reprints thirteen poems from his first, evidently the poet's choice among his earliest work. These thirteen are indicated by brackets in the table of contents; the later texts, which include only very slight revisions, are followed, but the poems themselves will be found in their original positions in *The Last Man.*

The uncollected poems have been drawn from periodicals of the forties and early fifties as well as from manuscript copies provided by the poet's father and by his long-time friend, Norris Getty. The present arrangement represents the editor's tentative estimate, based on incomplete evidence, of the approximate chronological order of their composition. Two or three appear to have been written after the publication of Kees' last book. The interest of the others seems to me sufficient warrant for their inclusion.

This edition would not have been possible without the kind permission and perfect cooperation of John A. Kees, the poet's father. To Norris Getty also I owe thanks for his great help.

Donald Justice

April, 1960

CONTENTS

THE LAST MAN

To Norris Getty & Maurice Johnson

SUBTITLE

We present for you this evening
A movie of death: observe
These scenes chipped celluloid
Reveals unsponsored and tax-free.

We request these things only:
All gum must be placed beneath the seats
Or swallowed quickly, all popcorn sacks
Must be left in the foyer. The doors
Will remain closed throughout
The performance. Kindly consult
Your programs: observe that
There are no exits. This is
A necessary precaution.

Look for no dialogue, or for the
Sound of any human voice: we have seen **fit**
To synchronize this play with
Squealings of pigs, slow sound of guns,
The sharp dead click
Of empty chocolatebar machines.
We say again: there are
No exits here, no guards to bribe,
No washroom windows.

No finis to the film unless
The ending is your own.
Turn off the lights, remind
The operator of his union card:
Sit forward, let the screen reveal
Your heritage, the logic of your destiny.

1936

Part One

STATEMENT WITH RHYMES

Plurality is all. I walk among the restaurants,
the theatres, the grocery stores; I ride the cars
and hear of Mrs. Bedford's teeth and Albuquerque,
strikes unsettled, someone's simply marvelous date,
news of the German Jews, the baseball scores,
storetalk and whoretalk, talk of wars. I turn
the pages of a thousand books to read
the names of Buddha, Malthus, Walker Evans, Stendhal,
   André Gide,
Ouspenski; note the terms: obscurantism,
factorize, fagaceous, endocarp; descend
the nervous stairs to hear the broken ends
of songs that float through city air.
In Osnabrück and Ogden, on the Passamaquoddy Bay,
in Ahmednagar, Waco (Neb.), in Santa Fé,
propelled by zeros, zinc, and zephyrs, always I'm pursued
by thoughts of what I am, authority, remembrance, food,
the letter on the mezzanine, the unemployed, dogs' lonely
   faces, pianos and decay.

Plurality is all. I sympathize, but cannot grieve
too long for those who wear their dialectics on their sleeves.
The pattern's one I sometimes rather like; there's really noth
   ing wrong
with it for some. But I should add: It doesn't wear for long,
before I push the elevator bell and quickly leave.

1938

4

TWO CITIES

Salt Lake
High spires of piety
No smoking on the grounds
Wide streets high wind
The hotel leaks orchestral sounds.

"Women and men pulled carts
Like oxen." Liquor sold
By package only. All the night
Wind again rain and unexpected cold.

The lake continues to recede; the girls
Forsake the faith; the Mormon hours pass.
We dutifully examine Brigham Young's
Gold inkwell (in a case of thumb-marked glass).

San Francisco
Beside the bay, observers penetrate
Distance upon distance, cloud on cloud,
Crayons of smoke that sketch blue sky
With gray appeals. We pause, stretched side by side,
Safe for the moment from the nudging crowd,
Laughter for strangeness, and old myths crisping in the grate.

These trinkets, essences that we have saved,
Sheathed valuables that hold us here
Where gull-cry, wave-wash, dash of listening sea
Stir memory and love, are suddenly
Minute survivors, permanent and clear.
—We must go back. Your eyes are mirrors, strangely grave.

THE SPEAKERS

"A equals X," says Mister One.
"A equals B," says Mister Two.
"A equals nothing under the sun
But A," says Mister Three. A few
Applaud; some wipe their eyes;
Some linger in the shade to see
One and Two in neat disguise
Decapitating Mister Three.

"This age is not entirely bad."
It's bad enough, God knows, but you
Should know Elizabethans had
Sweeneys and Mrs. Porters too.
The past goes down and disappears,
The present stumbles home to bed,
The future stretches out in years
That no one knows, and you'll be dead.

CORSAGE

Mind's residue is vein-violet
(old women with their stockings
hanging down)—gorged with
color and superb as light.
"The spangled riddle is twitter
and purr," the mussels murmured.
Then departed.
                     Of an evening,
in the empty park, sometimes I hear
the rustle of revival-meeting
pamphlets. Band music, with
surrealist trumpets, knifes the air.
Eagles with tusks perform in sieves.
The ectoptasm of Immanuel Kant unwittingly appears.

These bilious things, fracturing
the night's surface, swerve
into graphs, hanging like crags in jagged lines:
—profound, perfect, and
not without meaning.

THE INQUIRY

Do you wear a web over your wasted worth?
I wear a web

You fear the keyhole's splintered eye?
I fear the eye

Can you hear the worthless morning's mirth?
I hear it

The broken braying from whitening skies?
Yes I hear it yes

To spend the end and feed the fire
Is day's insistence, night's demand:
To pay the unrequested fare
And wave the wavering wand.

The streets are full of broken glass,
Sparkling in this frenzied noon.
With naked feet and bandaged eyes
You'll walk them—not just now, but soon.

THE SITUATION CLARIFIED

The frightened male librarian,
Young, though no longer so very young,
Exhibiting signs of incipient baldness,
Gyrated most considerately
Through all the latest books; was hung
By wires, pulled from rafters by a man
Who wore a striking wig and gave his name
(When sternly questioned by the police)
As Jones. "Jones is my name," he said.
A note of unmistakable bitterness,
Creeping into his voice,
Was singular. The whole affair
Was hushed up more or less immediately.
Pressure was brought to bear
(So persons of unquestionable integrity
Have testified) by an anonymous friend
Of the Carnegie family. And thus
Justice triumphed in the end,
Though not until dear Mrs. Cudlip-Finch
(Poor thing!) again experienced
Recurring twinges of her old, forgotten pain
In the duodenum.

VARIATIONS
ON A THEME BY JOYCE

The war is in words and the wood is the world
That turns beneath our rootless feet;
The vines that reach, alive and snarled,
Across the path where the sand is swirled,
Twist in the night. The light lies flat.
The war is in words and the wood is the world.

The rain is ruin and our ruin rides
The swiftest winds; the wood is whorled
And turned and smoothed by the turning tides.
—There is rain in the woods, slow rain that breeds
The war in the words. The wood is the world.
This rain is ruin and our ruin rides.

The war is in words and the wood is the world,
Sourceless and seized and forever filled
With green vines twisting on wood more gnarled
Than dead men's hands. The vines are curled
Around these branches, crushed and killed.
The war is in words and the wood is the world.

PRAISE TO THE MIND

Praise to the mind
That slowly grows
In solid breadth, that knows
Its varied errors, shows
And will admit
Its witlessness.

Praise to the single mind
That sees no street
Run through this world, complete,
That does not meet,
Bending at end,
Remorselessly, its source.

Praise to the mind
That moves toward meaning,
Kindness; mixes keenness
With routine of
Grace, has space,
And finds its place.

WHAT THE SPIDER HEARD

Will there be time for eggnogs and eclogues
In the place where we're going?
Said the spider to the fly.

    I think not, said the fly.
    I think not, sang the chorus.
    I think not, said a stranger
    Who mysteriously happened by.

Will they beat me and treat me the way they did here,
In the place where we're going?
Asked the spider of the fly.

    It is likely, said the fly.
    Very likely, sang the chorus.
    Extremely likely, said the stranger,
    With an eager gleam in his eye.

O, why go there when we know there is nothing there but fear
At this place where we're going?
Said the spider to the fly.

    What a question! said the fly.
    What a question! sang the chorus.
    What a question! said the stranger,
    Leering slightly at the spider,
    Winking slyly at the fly.

WHITE COLLAR BALLAD

There are lots of places to go:
Guaranteed headaches at every club,
Plush-and-golden cinemas that always show
How cunningly the heroine and hero rub.
Put on your hat, put on your gloves.
But there isn't any love, there isn't any love.

There are endless things we could do:
Walk around the block, watch the skaters whirl,
Promenade the park or see the newest zoo,
Plan for the future in a sensible world.
The water boils on the stove,
But there isn't any love, there isn't any love.

Our best friends lived in the house next door.
Went around to call on them the other day,
But they hadn't left an address or a word before
They packed their bags and moved away.
We could call on the people on the floor above,
But there wouldn't be any love, there wouldn't be any love.

It didn't use to be like this at all.
You wanted lots of money and I got it somehow.
Once it was Summer. Here it's almost Fall.
It isn't any season now.
There are seasons in the future to be thinking of,
But there won't be any love, there won't be any love.

FOR MY DAUGHTER

Looking into my daughter's eyes I read
Beneath the innocence of morning flesh
Concealed, hintings of death she does not heed.
Coldest of winds have blown this hair, and mesh
Of seaweed snarled these miniatures of hands;
The night's slow poison, tolerant and bland,
Has moved her blood. Parched years that I have seen
That may be hers appear: foul, lingering
Death in certain war, the slim legs green.
Or, fed on hate, she relishes the sting
Of others' agony; perhaps the cruel
Bride of a syphilitic or a fool.
These speculations sour in the sun.
I have no daughter. I desire none.

THE SCENE OF THE CRIME

There should have been some witness there, accusing—
Women with angry mouths and burning eyes
To fill the house with unforgiving cries;
But there was only silence for abuse.

There should have been exposure—more than curtains
Drawn, the stairway coiling to the floor
Where no one walked, the sheeted furniture,
And one thin line of light beneath the door.

Walking the stairs to reach that room, a pool
Of blood swam in his thought, a hideous guide
That led him on and vanished in the hall.
There should have been damnation. But, inside,
Only an old man clawed the bed, and drooled,
Whispering, "Murderer!" before he died.

FOR H. V. (1901–1927)

I remember the clumsy surgery: the face
Scarred out of recognition, ruined and not his own.
Wax hands fattened among pink silk and pinker roses.
The minister was in fine form that afternoon.

I remember the ferns, the organ faintly out of tune,
The gray light, the two extended prayers,
Rain falling on stained glass; the pallbearers,
Selected by the family, and none of them his friends.

Part Two

JUNE 1940

"Yet these elegies are to this generation in no sense consolatory.

They may be to the next. All a poet can do today is warn."
    "The old Lie: Dulce et decorum est
    Pro patria mori."
                                                —WILFRED OWEN

It is summer, and treachery blurs with the sounds of midnight,
The lights blink off at the closing of a door,
And I am alone in a worn-out town in wartime,
Thinking of those who were trapped by hysteria once before.

Flaubert and Henry James and Owen,
Bourne with his crooked back, Rilke and Lawrence, Joyce—
Gun-shy, annoyers, sick of the kill, the watchers,
Suffered the same attack till it broke them or left its scars.

Now the heroes of March are the sorriest fools of April:
The beaters of drums, the flag-kissing men, whose eyes
Once saw the murder, are washing it clean, accusing:
"You are the cowards! All that we told you before was lies!"

It is summer again, the evening is warm and silent.
The windows are dark and the mountains are miles away.
And the men who were haters of war are mounting the plat-
    forms.
An idiot wind is blowing; the conscience dies.

AFTER THE TRIAL

Hearing the judges' well-considered sentence,
The prisoner saw long plateaus of guilt,
And thought of all the dismal furnished rooms
The past assembled, the eyes of parents
Staring through walls as though forever
To condemn and wound his innocence.

And if I raise my voice, protest my innocence,
The judges won't revoke their sentence.
I could stand screaming in this box forever,
Leaving them deaf to everything but guilt;
All the machinery of law devised by parents
Could not be stopped though fire swept the rooms.

Whenever my thoughts move to all those rooms
I sat alone in, capable of innocence,
I know now I was not alone, that parents
Always were there to speak the hideous sentence:
"You are our son; be good; we know your guilt;
We stare through walls and see your thoughts forever."

Sometimes I wished to go away forever;
I dreamt of strangers and of stranger rooms
Where every corner held the light of guilt.
Why do the judges stare? I saw no innocence
In them when they pronounced the sentence;
I heard instead the believing voice of parents.

I can remember evenings when my parents,
Settling my future happily forever,
Would frown before they spoke the sentence:

"Someday the time will come to leave these rooms
Where, under our watchful eyes, you have been innocent;
Remember us before you seize the world of guilt."

Their eyes burn. How can I deny my guilt
When I am guilty in the sight of parents?
I cannot think that even they were innocent.
At least I shall not have to wait forever
To be escorted to the silent rooms
Where darkness promises a final sentence.

We walk forever to the doors of guilt,
Pursued by our own sentences and eyes of parents,
Never to enter innocent and quiet rooms.

THE PARTY

The obscene hostess, mincing in the hall,
Gathers the guests around a crystal ball.
It is on the whole an exciting moment;
Mrs. Lefevre stares with her one good eye;
A friendly abdomen rubs against one's back;
"Interesting," a portly man is heard to sigh.

A somewhat unconvincing oriental leers
Redundantly; into the globe he peers,
Mutters a word or two and stands aside.
The glass grows cloudy with sulphorous fumes;
Beads rattle, latecomers giggle near the door.
A scene forms in the glass; silence invades the rooms.

The oriental glances up, conceals surprise
At such immediate success. Our eyes
Stare at the planes that fill the swelling globe,
Smoke-blue; blood, shelltorn faces. Suddenly a drum
Begins its steady beat, pursues us even here:
Death, and death again, and all the wars to come.

A CORNUCOPIA FOR DAILY USE

Publish these perils in a colder ice:
Lean as some half-starved animal,
The trap's teeth breaking through the bone;
The bloodless face, tempting a death-mask;
A dream of retching, memories of an ether cone,
The ripped hand, twisted in a vise.

BONES. The Greek dictionary is there by the cleaver.
SAMBO. Swell of Lillian to send us these fig newtons.

They came considerably unlike swallows;
Fat eyes that measured outlines of a noon
More damned than ever Mr. Frambach
(Who even now disturbs our narrative),
Early to murder and a corpse too soon.
Fog drifted slowly from the hollows.

A.E.H. (drowsily). Were you a rose-lipped lass when I lifted
the sky and shouldered the can?

JESSUP (humbly). I always use the three-for-a-dollar kind
myself, sir.

Here is the Sunday resurrection in a room
With morning painted coldly on the walls you passed.
The sunlight strained against the sill; the breeze
Was free of winter and the night before.
Yet, when your face moved silently across the glass,
Memory and blood proclaimed the rank disease.

FISHER-BARHAM. My heart leaps up when I behold.

21

MUMFORD (a dwarf). One operation and it's as gleaming and shiny as new. (*Leers*)

Give us, for God's sake, a hosanna or a good-luck charm,
A slogan infallible as death; give us a death
Meaningful, at least, as Mr. Frambach's, and tell us why
His end was normal when they snapped his arm,
Kicked him down darkened stairs (fresh blood against
The banister) and left him there to die.

TWO STRANGERS. We have built Jerusalem in England's green and pleasant land.

AN OLD MAN. I think I see a new process here, a beginning perhaps; the beginning of the end.

RESORT

The empty and disordered porches hold
The summer's burdened and uneasy death.
Eyes of the ruined boarders are unmasked;
The stairway sags a last time until Spring.

A wind that ushers winter chills the beach,
Blowing the papers and the sacks above the sand,
Whining through all the empty and abandoned rooms,
Banging the shutters no one thought to close.

This is the record: several outraged guests
Who left in early June, no one knew why;
The woman with the feeble-minded child;
The man with obscene postcards in his room;

The clerk that opened everybody's mail;
The woman who put sugar in her beer;
One frame-up, one divorce, one minor theft.
"Goodbye, goodbye! We shall be back again next year!"

THE CATERPILLAR AND THE MEN
FROM CAMBRIDGE

"The most celebrated of all caterpillars, whose history is in part recorded in Professor Lloyd Morgan's Habit and Instinct, *page 41, was striped yellow and black and was seized by one of the professor's chickens. Being offensive in taste to the chicken he was rejected. Henceforth the chicken refrained from seizing similar caterpillars. Why? Because the sight of such a caterpillar, a part that is of the whole sight-seize-taste context of the original experience, now excites the chicken in a way sufficiently like that in which the whole context did, for the seizing at least not to occur, whether the tasting (in images) does or not."*

—THE MEANING OF MEANING

> Professor Lloyd Morgan's chicken dropped
> The proffered caterpillar with irritable haste.
> It made no attempt to seize similar larvae
> Because of the creature's objectionable taste.
>
> This simple example, say Ogden and Richards,
> Explains how some writing, once studied, does more.
> For merely a part of the context will cause us
> To react in the way we reacted before.
>
> But what of the chicken? Is Lloyd Morgan living?
> More important than that is the unpleasant fate
> Of the worm. Did it suffer? Is anything heard
> Of this martyr to science, this pitiful bait?

ON A PAINTING BY ROUSSEAU

The clouds seem neater than the trees.
The sky, like faded overalls,
Breaks the distances of sight;
And shadow that defines the curb
Shelters the silhouette of dog
Who, waiting patiently beneath
The amazing carriage with tangerine wheels,
Is eyeless, though he seems to sense
The black Chihuahua that the pavement grows.

The street is bare. The hooves and mane
Of the posing horse and his speckled flanks
Flow back to the six in the cart he draws:
The idiot aunt and the girl in white
(A ventriloquist's doll with a colorless wig),
And a sexless figure upon whose lap
A beast is squatting, macabre, blurred.

These four and the one in the yellow hat
Regard us with eyes like photographs
That have been shown us long ago.
—All but the man in the driver's seat,
His wax hands fastened on the reins,
Who, from the corners of his eyes,
Watches the horse he does not trust.

AUNT ELIZABETH

They lean in frames along the fading wall,
The hideous ancestors. While Aunt Elizabeth,
Imprisoned by *National Geographics,* cats, and air
Enclosing dead poinsettia plants, rocks slowly in the chair
Her mother died in. "And when the 'phone rang, Paul,"
She says, "I answered. There was no one there;
There was no one there at all!"

Her past is rearranged by hardening arteries,
The neighbors' dogs, ruining her flower bed,
Nieces' abortions, failing profits, and the dead, of course,
Their nerveless eyes along the wall. They were well fed,
Expiring quietly among the parlor furniture or in some room
Upstairs, the older ones; two of them shot
In wars abroad; one of the girls
Stabbed herself with a paperknife; but gently;
The wound healed.
                              "But you don't understand
The way it was!" says Aunt Elizabeth. "It's always that way.
I answer, and there's no one there!"

The window glasses out the afternoon.
Tall April weeds hold in the crumbling walk;
A broken trellis sags where yellow vines once grew.
And there has been no telephone in years.

"No one," she says, and rocks, and coughs,
Imprisoned by these photographs and memories.

26

EARLY WINTER

Memory of summer is winter's consciousness.
Sitting or walking or merely standing still,
Earning a living or watching the snow fall,
I am remembering the sun on sidewalks in a warmer place,
A small hotel and a dead girl's face;
I think of these in this higher altitude, staring West.

But the room is cold, the words in the books are cold;
And the question of whether we get what we ask for
Is absurd, unanswered by the sound of an unlatched door
Rattling in wind, or the sound of snow on roofs, or glare
Of the winter sun. What we have learned is not what we were
    told.
I watch the snow, feel for the heartbeat that is not there.

TO THE NORTH

If I, like others in their burrowings,
Could find some acre of the past to praise,
There might be substitutes for noise and blurs:
The comforts of asylum, strict, assured,
That nourish when the light dies in the glass.
But the mind must crouch, suspicious, veer away,
And focus into idiot light the days
Of other whippings, exiles, sicknesses
Where the horror of history from cave
To camp to the coffins of yesterday
Burns to a single ash.
                Where is the grave
Of Time? What would you picture for decay?
A horse's hoof, white bones, a lifeless tree,
Cold hemispheres, dried moss, and a blue wave
Breaking at noon on shores you will not see.

SCREAM AS YOU LEAVE

Restricted journeys and steam-heated dreams,
The mothball moment dropping like an iron
On crowded fringe of ground that hinges heart
And mind, suggesting codas to the start
Of twenty ends. The statues by the pool
Have varicose veins. Damp weather does it.

Consult the local seers as blue x-rays
Deposit profiles of the worms who ate
The rector's aphorism in a single swallow.
It happened on this weathered street, beneath a yellow
Pool of oil, where Christian Scientists cross fearlessly,
Their souls bound up in packages, like knobs.

And trapped among the toothpicks and the phallic balloons
Where minor Caesars fell outrageously,
Impromptu unicorns enact ballets,
Applauded by bourgeoisie in negligée.
What are these dying blackbirds doing here?
The weather wrinkles to a shrunken end.

WHEN THE LEASE IS UP

Walk the horses down the hill
Through the darkening groves;
Pat their rumps and leave the stall;
Even the eyeless cat perceives
Things are not going well.

Fasten the lock on the drawingroom door,
Cover the tables with sheets:
This is the end of the swollen year
When even the sound of the rain repeats:
The lease is up, the time is near.

Pull the curtains to the sill,
Darken the rooms, cut all the wires.
Crush the embers as they fall
From the dying fires:
Things are not going well.

Part Three

HENRY JAMES AT NEWPORT

For Ann

And shores and strands and naked piers,
Sunset on waves, orange laddering the blue,
White sails on headlands, cool
Wide curving bay, dim landward distances
Dissolving in the property of local air.

Viterbo, Bagdad, Carcassonne—
They play upon the mind, the eyes again,
Although these back verandas, resolutely prim,
Say *Quakers, Roger Williams*—murmurs of the past—
While special staircase ghosts return,
Known voices in the old brown rooms:
"People don't do those things."
The pictures huddle in the frames.

Removed from those blank days
In which the margin is consumed,
The palace sites stare seaward, pure, *blasé,*
Remember the detached, the casually disqualified,
The mild cosmopolites whose ivory dream
Found no successors, quietly embalmed.
They nursed nostalgia on the sun-warmed rocks,
Exquisite, sterile, easily distressed,
Thought much of Paris; died
While he lived out their deaths.

Shores, strands, white sails and naked piers,

Wide curving bay and landward distances.
Thoughts of the dispossessed on summer afternoons.
The sails are tattered and the shrubs are dead.
The stone-walled fields are featureless.

STALE WEATHER

Indelible canyons yawn their green
Confusion through the empty air,
And from the pleasant tear-drenched scene,
High-class assassins dash everywhere.

The rusty bird sang a song about graves.

Red lips and bleeding lips, wet lips and pale
Murmur, "How charming!" as the starving are hung.
Reversible horses leak gallons of ale
While fluttering mothers devour their young.

The rusty bird sang a song about graves.

A dead fish floats voluptuously
Across the landscape, clear and blue;
Its neon mouth flashes, "Vote for McGee,"
While over its head is a halo or two.

The rusty bird sang a song about graves.

The breasts are caking, the manna's stale,
The voices fade as the evening dies.
Out of a cloud comes a hollow wail
And a purple stain spreads over the skies.

The rusty bird sang a song about graves.

MIDNIGHT

When curdling mists disturb the sight's
Intensity, when clouds of frozen light
Blur inward, imminent and clear,
This vacant street, your enemy, will drain
All solace for a bastard audience.
Down passages, past milestones, far
And under, fragments, odds and ends
Of you, like Bloom's in Dublin, drift and sway
Unfocused; separate where the sky bends,
Rigid with a sense of sin, they penetrate and stay.
While landscapes, dangerously still,
Re-echo with indifference and hate,
The paths are guarded by the violent, who wait
Impatiently. Black clouds hang on the hill.

—The mist lifts. Near your bed the moonlight carves
Blue scrolls that twist upon the floor.
Outside, through summer darkness, someone calls.
The leaves stir. This is your familiar room,
With your familiar odor lingering and real,
The known disturbance nightly in the hall,
Worn rug, the broken chandelier,
The flowered paper peeling from the walls.

OBITUARY

Boris is dead. The fatalist parrot
No longer screams warnings to Avenue A.
He died last week on a rainy day.
He is sadly missed. His spirit was rare.

The cage is empty. The unhooked chain,
His pitiful droppings, the sunflower seeds,
The brass sign, "Boris," are all that remain.
His irritable body is under the weeds.

Like Eliot's world, he went out with a whimper;
Silent for days, with his appetite gone,
He watched the traffic flow by, unheeding,
His universe crumbling, his heart a stone.

No longer will Boris cry, "Out, brief candle!"
Or "Down with tyranny, hate, and war!"
To astonished churchgoers and businessmen.
Boris is dead. The porch is a tomb.
And a black wreath decorates the door.

FUGUE

When the light
Begins to fail,
Many now alive
Will fall.
Falling night
Will darken drives,
Spread the darkness
Over all.

Though the sun
Is blinding now,
Spreading heat
On grass and skin,
Minutes tick
With steady beat,
Saying sun
Will soon be gone.

Light will fail,
Alive will fall;
Sun that blinded
Will be gone.
Heat will vanish
With the sun.
Falling night
Will cover all.

INSECTAE BORINQUENSES

... reared from aceitillo,
resting on sugar-cane at Toa Baja,
riddling the leaves at Mayaguez,

on sea-grape at Patillas
(integument entirely black: no scales,
short silvery hairs).

Or alone in decayed wood,
in tamarind seed pods, under
dead bark of the yuma palm, or beneath

dry seaweed, feeding on sand fleas
from here to Mona Island,
rotting wet fish on the endless sands.

Or from mango fruit in Bayamon,
in salt lagoons at Guanica,
attacking peppers, burrowing into gladiolus bulbs,

nesting in stumps, attacking caterpillars,
carrying a legless spider at Coloso—
thousands upon thousands—

restless forever, and quite indomitable.

THE FORESTS

And the traveller
stumbles in darkness, hearing
beasts in the forest, fearing
the pitfalls, pitch-black ditches,
the brambles. Dread
in his heart: and the air
whispering death:
and his breath strangled.

But along the path:
a torch! The soaked pine
blazes, blinding the night.
The grateful seizing, and he feels
the fear half-gone, and sees
the pathway clear. And then at last
the sun's slow rise from night:
cold fragile light that streaks
across the timber. And the way
uncertain still. All night
he'd known that they were there:
knew they were waiting there:
waiting for him. But then at dawn,
emerging from the forest,
he felt his heart at peace.
The day! Alive with brightness!
Wonderful to be alive!

Then he thought of the other forests beyond . . .

THE VIEW OF THE CASTLE

The castle is mortgaged now, my dear,
The mortgage is overdue:
The moat, the tower, the beautiful yards,
The silverware and the frightening guards;
Although it's still on the postal cards,
The castle is mortgaged now, my dear;
They whisper its days are few.

The castle's been cracking for years, my dear,
And has not been properly cleaned;
The rooms are draughty and bring on colds,
The pantries are covered with unpleasant moulds,
It's thought rather queer the foundation holds
After so many years, my dear;
And it's best not to speak of the beams.

The princesses were whores, my dear,
The princesses were whores;
The queen looks on with unconcern,
The king tries hard to seem strong and stern,
Yet neither of them was much startled to learn
That the princesses were whores, my dear,
And the prince was covered with sores.

This is the castle then, my dear,
With its justly famous view.
There are other historic sights in store—
Battlegrounds, parks we might explore,
The hundreds of monuments to war;
Now that you've seen the castle, my dear,
We'll see them before we're through.

TO A CONTEMPORARY

J'ai plus de souvenirs que si j' avais mille ans.

—BAUDELAIRE

Memories rich as Proust's or Baudelaire's are yours,
You think: snarled ravelings of doubt at evening scents
Of women, dazed with pleasure, whose white legs and arms
Once coiled with languor around you; arguments
With undistinguished friends, their bigotries each year
More fixed. Lamps in the mist that light strange faces fill
Your nights; your fingers drum upon the table as you stare,
Uncertain, at the floor. *Un vieux boudoir?* Impossible!
You frequently compare yourself to those whose memories
Are cruel, contemptible, like naked bone.

Yet, is there anything in this rank richness warm
Or permanent? At every climax, trapped, alone,
You seem to be a helpless passenger that drifts
On some frail boat; and with oblivious ease,
As from a distance, watch yourself
Disintegrate in foaming seas.

HOMAGE TO ARTHUR WALEY

Seattle weather: it has rained for weeks in this town,
The dampness breeding moths and a gray summer.
I sit in the smoky room reading your book again,
My eyes raw, hearing the trains steaming below me
In the wet yard, and I wonder if you are still alive.
Turning the worn pages, reading once more:
"By misty waters and rainy sands, while the yellow dusk
   thickens."

THE CITY AS HERO

For those whose voices cry from ruins
For those who die in the dark alone
For those who walk the ruined streets

Here in your evening

The chimneys are empty of smoke
These squares of darkness are windows
The soundless wires stretch across the sky
Stillness of air
Under cold stars
And near the dry river
An old man without shadow walks alone

Upon pillows of darkness
Here is your evening

What words What answers now
What memories What ruined harbors?

LINES FOR AN ALBUM

Over the river and through the woods
To grandmother's house we go . . .

She waits behind the bolted door,
Her withered face in thirty pieces,
While blood runs thin, and memory,
An idiot without a name,
Recalls the snows of eighty years,
The daughter whose death was unexplained,
Darkness, blue veins, and broken leases.
Grandmother waits behind the door
(Sight dims beyond the curtain folds)
With her toothless smile and enuresis.

Over the river and through the woods
To grandmother's house we go . . .

THE SMILES OF THE BATHERS

The smiles of the bathers fade as they leave the water,
And the lover feels sadness fall as it ends, as he leaves his love.
The scholar, closing his book as the midnight clocks strike, is
    hollow and old;
The pilot's relief on landing is no release.
These perfect and private things, walling us in, have imper-
    fect and public endings—
Water and wind and flight, remembered words and the act of
    love
Are but interruptions. And the world, like a beast, impatient
    and quick,
Waits only for those that are dead. No death for you. You
    are involved.

THE FALL OF THE MAGICIANS

FOR ANN

Part One

EIGHT VARIATIONS

1.

Prurient tapirs gamboled on our lawns,
But that was quite some time ago.
Now one is accosted by asthmatic bulldogs,
Sluggish in the hedges, ruminant.

Moving through ivy in the park
Near drying waterfalls, we open every gate;
But that grave, shell-white unicorn is gone.
The path is strewn with papers to the street.

Numbers that once were various
Regarded us, were thought significant, significant
Enough to bring reporters to the scene.
But now the bell strikes one, strikes one,

Strikes one—monotonous and tired.

Or clicks like a sad valise.

2. *Note to Be Left on the Table*
This ghost of yours, padding about the upper halls,
Given to fright-wigs Burbage might have worn,
Moaning in doorways, jumping out at maids,
Has not convinced me even yet. Can this be you?
Your life was frightening enough, but this
Poor pallid counterpart who fuddles in its role
Is inexcusable. Go haunt the houses of the girls
You once infected, or the men who bore
Your company far oftener than I; annoy the others
For a change. Is this, my house, the medieval hell

You took to at the grave's edge, years ago,
After a dozen other hells had burned themselves away,
Or are we purgatory here? If not,
You make it one. I give you until noon.

3.

Ruined travelers in sad trousseaux
Roost on my doorstep, indolent and worn.
Not one of them fulfills despised Rousseau's
Predictions. Perhaps they are waiting to be born.
If so, the spot's been badly chosen.
This is a site for posthumous investigations,
Pillows stuffed with nettles, charnal notions:
Apoplectic executioners, bungled incisions.
Indeed, our solitary midwife fondles the hemlock.

We welcomed one poor hackneyed Christ,
Sad bastard, croaking of pestilence. The basement
Holds him now. He has not as yet arisen.
The tickets are ready; the line forms on the right.
Justice and virtue, you will find, have been amazingly pre-
    served

4.

As water from a dwindling resevoir
Uncovers mossy stones, new banks of silt,
So every minute that I spend with you reveals
New flaws, new features, new intangibles.
We have been sitting here for hours—
"I spent that summer in Madrid,
The winter on the coast of France—
The Millotsons were there, and Farnsworth.

My work has perished with the rest
Of Europe, gone, all gone. We will not see the end."

You said goodbye, and your perfume
Lingered for hours. At first it seemed
Like summer dying there, then rank and sharp.

And yet I did not air the room.

5.
Among Victorian beadwork and the smell of plush,
The owls, stuffed and marvelously sinister,
Glare from dark corners, waiting for the night.
High up, the moose's passive eyes explore
Candles, unlit, within cut-glass. A door
Is opened, and you enter with a look
You might have saved for Pliny or the Pope.

The furniture has shrunk now thirty years
Have passed (with talent thinning out, and words
Gone dead), and mouths of friends in photographs
Display their hopeful and outmoded smiles.
You counted on at least a sputter of nostalgia,
However fretful. That was a mistake. Even the moose
Regards you with a tired, uncomprehending stare.

6.
Signboards commemorate their resting place.
The graveless of another century
Came and were conquered; now their bones
Are dust where idiot highways run.
Land in their eyes, unquiet ancestors
(On fences yellow signs clang in the wind)

Unstirred by suns drying the brown weeds
Above them now in parched and caking land.

But when they speak of you, they feel the need
Of voices polished and revised by history,
The martial note, words framed in capitals.

It is good to be deaf in a deafening time
With the sky gone colorless, while the dead
Thunder breaks, a cracked dish, out of the mind.

7.
The eye no longer single: where the bowl,
Dead in the thickened darkness, swelled with light,
Transformed the images and moved the artist's hand,
Becomes a framework for our mania.

And haunts the stairway. Friends depart,
Taking their last look from the roof,
Saying goodnight and carrying their view
Of grapes the model ate in Paris years ago.

Blue in the morning, green some afternoons;
The night, ambiguous, forgets the signature.

The dust in attics settled and his stove
Grew cold. About the model nothing much is known.

It ends the wall and complements the view
Of chimneys. And it hides a stain.

8.
And when your beauty, washed away
In impure streams with my desire,

Is only topic for ill-mannered minds,
Gifted and glassy with exact recall,
Gossip and rancid footnotes, or remote despair,
Let ruined weather perish in the streets
And let the world's black lying flag come down.

Only in calendars that mark no Spring
Can there be weather in the mind
That moves to you again as you are now:
Tired after love and silent in this house,
Your back turned to me, quite alone,
Standing with one hand raised to smooth your hair,
At a small window, green with rain.

THE CONVERSATION
IN THE DRAWING ROOM

—That spot of blood on the drawing room wall,
No larger than a thumbnail when I looked a moment ago,
Is spreading, Cousin Agatha, and growing brighter.

Nonsense. The oriole warbles in the sunlight.
The fountains gush luxuriantly above the pool.
The weather is ideal: on the paths a sheen
Of summer provides a constant delight.
I am thinking of affiliating with a new theosophist group.

—Once you could hide it with a nickel.
Now it strangely assumes the shape and size of a palm,
And puts out fingers, Cousin Agatha. Look, examine it!

Some aberration of the wallpaper, no doubt.
Did you have an omelette for lunch, and asparagus?
Mrs. Pisgah's husband spoke from the beyond during the
    séance
Last night at Madame Irani's. He seemed to have a cold.
The tambourine did not function with its usual zest.

And a wrist, Cousin Agatha, and an arm!
Like those maps in a cinema that spread
Like wind blowing over a field of wheat, Cousin Agatha!

I have warned you, Hobart, about reading *The Turn of the
    Screw*
And that story of Balzac's, whatever the name of it is,
Just before retiring. They always have a decidedly bad effect
    upon you.

I believe I will put another aspirin in the lily's vase.
And now I must go to take my nap in the sunroom.

—Cousin Agatha, it moves like a fish, wet,
Wet like a fish, becomes a moving thing
That spreads and reaches from the wall!

I cannot listen to you any more just now, Hobart.
Kindly speak to Marie about the place cards for this evening.
Ah, there is the oriole again; how beautiful the view
From this window!—Yet why, one wonders, must Hobart begin
Gasping and screaming in such a deplorable fashion
There in the drawing room? It is scarcely considerate.
Youthful animal spirits, one supposes, combined
With a decided taste for the macabre. Where is the barbital?
Marie can never learn to leave it here, by the incense burner.
Ah, now he has stopped and only thrashes about, rather feebly,
    on the floor.
It is a beautiful afternoon; I will get up about three-fifteen.
Everything is blissfully quiet now; I am ready for sleep.

THE CONTOURS OF FIXATION

The stoned dogs crawl back through the blood,
Through the conquered weather, through the wet silk light,
To disenchanted masters who are not quite dead.

Like severed heads of a dead age
They gasp in the square, in the alleys of dusk.
Explanations are posted on the shattered walls.

The moon illuminates a cenotaph.
"All is insanity," the dogs conclude,
Yet the odor of blood has a certain appeal.

Their pain soaks eyes on every balcony.
"Forbear, refrain, be scrupulous"—dogs' admonitions,
Sad and redundant, paraphernalia of goodbye,

Hang in the sulphured air like promises of girls.
Then silence. Down the street the lights go dead.
One waits, one waits. And then the guns sound on another
    hill.

MOVING TARGET

The tone has changed. Who used to come,
Savage at nightfall toward the daylight house,
Is he who now aims nothing at that hymn
Buried as enemy, and without peace,
On a bad yesterday. Who used to damn
The rusty scissors and the crooked lease
Is you; and yet the praise is lame.
Here is a faithless map for all your praise.

Applauded monsters, issuing their lies,
Leap from the mirrors of your home
Toward the late news, accompanied by screams.
The crêpe is a good idea, also the cross.
But he who used to speak in pitiless light is dumb.

THE PATIENT IS RALLYING

Difficult to recall an emotion that is dead,
Particularly so among these unbelieved fanfares
And admonitions from a camouflaged sky.

I should have remained burdened with destinations
Perhaps, or stayed quite drunk, or obeyed
The undertaker, who was fairly charming, after all.

Or was there a room like that one, worn
With our whispers, and a great tree blossoming
Outside blue windows, warm rain blowing in the night?

There seems to be some doubt. No doubt, however,
Of the chilled and empty tissues of the mind
—Cold, cold, a great gray winter entering—
Like spines of air, frozen in an ice cube.

REPORT OF THE MEETING

The scientists removed their coats and hats
And climbed upon an antiseptic stage.
A toothless lion suffered in his cage,
Ignoring them. The men of science sat.

One breathed an introductory gasp,
Stood up and fastened glasses to his nose,
And told the crowd—before he grew verbose—
The Life Elixir lay within their grasp.

"We hold this meeting here today
So you may see this ancient lion fed
The Life Elixir." As an afterthought he said,
"It has a bitter taste." He told them of the way

The scientists poured liquids into vats
For years uncountable; examined sperms,
Blood, sputum, knee-jerk, heartbeat, germs;
Invented baffling mazes where white rats

Learned methods of success or went insane;
Experimented with the brains of larks;
Filled notebooks with a million puzzling marks;
And doped retarded monkeys with cocaine.

"The years went by in study without rest
In search of the Elixir that would bring
Eternal life to man and beast; and then one Spring,"
He said, "we were rewarded with success."

This ended his remarks. Applause.
The men of science went within the cage

And fed the lion, who had reached an age
Of weariness and trust. (They had, however, dulled his claws.)

The beast on whom the remedy was tried
Watched them file out with tolerant disdain,
Yawned at the crowd and shook his mane,
Grew cross, dozed fitfully, and died.

Silence; and then a thousand metronomes
Ticked violently, the air blurred, people hissed
And took their leave; some mumbled, "Fake." The scientists
Returned, annoyed and puzzled, to their homes,

Where they wrote monographs on every phase
Of the affair, constructed graphs and charts and plans,
Cut up the lion, placed its parts in pans
And did not venture on the streets for days.

Part Two

ROBINSON

The dog stops barking after Robinson has gone.
His act is over. The world is a gray world,
Not without violence, and he kicks under the grand piano,
The nightmare chase well under way.

The mirror from Mexico, stuck to the wall,
Reflects nothing at all. The glass is black.
Robinson alone provides the image Robinsonian.

Which is all of the room—walls, curtains,
Shelves, bed, the tinted photograph of Robinson's first wife,
Rugs, vases, panatellas in a humidor.
They would fill the room if Robinson came in.

The pages in the books are blank,
The books that Robinson has read. That is his favorite chair,
Or where the chair would be if Robinson were here.

All day the phone rings. It could be Robinson
Calling. It never rings when he is here.

Outside, white buildings yellow in the sun.
Outside, the birds circle continuously
Where trees are actual and take no holiday.

THE AMBASSADORS

No eyes. No light. The one chilled and imperfect hand
Claws at the spot where banisters had been,
Or finds, eventually, the smoothness of a wall.
Sweats like a brow where palmists viewed a tourist's health,
Turns a black page. This is the way
We believe we learn again. This is the way we learn
Something.

     Smile without mirrors at a point in space
Defined by one sharp perfect landscape in the mind
That holds its focus for a second and then fails,
And will not, ever, probably, be quite so sharp again.

Turns a black page . . . Learn sunlight
If you can: the bottom of the pit
Whirls in this quiet and is dark,
Is cold, is all the places you have never seen,
Is everything the doctors did not say,
Is cold, with water running down the sides.

Chains drag through gravel. Nothing is left
But the desire to be something you are not—
To have been wholly evil or less evil than you were,
To have returned exactly as you left
Before the preparations for this darkness were arranged.
To find the lips to say, "At least it was a life."
The legless men on city sidewalks hurry by
On wheels of rollerskates; and what they know
Shrivels the paper flowers, near their genitals.

It is a warm morning. This is part of the world.
There are the victories and the defeats to redistinguish.
Is this all? Is this the way we learn
Something? This is the way we learn.

DYNAMITE FOR OPERAS

After the red rugs of the palaces,
Roofs of those great hotels, views of the sea,
I seem to be back in this familiar room again.
Brought here, perhaps. It was February when I left.

It is hard to touch death while part-time roles
In melodramas of decay provide the time
For one to smile eccentrically in dressing rooms.
I never smiled much here. Farewell, colleagues of the sublime!
I greet the welcome papers blowing down a street
I know too well. Someone has wound the clock,
Which ticks like a bomb, and is not culpable.

To wake again and know that time
Grinds on, grinds on, is what I missed,
Or so the blowing curtains seem to say.
That emptiness was richer than this emptiness.
Too rich. I liked it all the less for that.
A chilly landscape tightens up the mind.

SESTINA: TRAVEL NOTES

Directed by the eyes of others,
Blind to the long, deceptive voyage,
We walked across the bridge in silence
And said "Goodnight," and paused, and walked away.
Ritual of apology and burden:
The evening ended; not a soul was harmed.

But then I thought: we all are harmed
By the indifference of others;
Being corrupt, corruptible, they burden
All who would vanish on some questioned voyage,
Tunneling through the longest way away
To maps of bitterness and silence.

We are concerned with that destructive silence
Impending in the dark, that never harms
Us till it strikes, washing the past away.
Remote from intrigues of the others,
We must chart routes that ease the voyage,
Clear passageways and lift the burden.

But where are routes? Who names the burden?
The night is gifted with a devious silence
That names no promises of voyage
Without contagion and the syllables of harm.
—I see ahead the hands of others
In frantic motion, warning me away.

To pay no heed, and walk away
Is easy; but the familiar burden
Of a later time, when certainties of others

Assume the frigid shapes of silence
And build new winters, echoing harm,
May banish every passageway for voyage.

You knew before the fear of voyage,
You saw before the hands that warned away,
You heard before the voices trained to harm
Listeners grown weak through loss and burdens.
Even in city streets at noon that silence
Waited for you, but not, you thought, for others.

Storms will break silence. Seize on harm,
Play idiot or seer to others, make the burden
Theirs, though no voyage is, no tunnel, door, nor way.

FIVE VILLANELLES

1.

The crack is moving down the wall.
Defective plaster isn't all the cause.
We must remain until the roof falls in.

It's mildly cheering to recall
That every building has its little flaws.
The crack is moving down the wall.

Here in the kitchen, drinking gin,
We can accept the damndest laws.
We must remain until the roof falls in.

And though there's no one here at all,
One searches every room because
The crack is moving down the wall.

Repairs? But how can one begin?
The lease has warnings buried in each clause.
We must remain until the roof falls in.

These nights one hears a creaking in the hall,
The sort of thing that gives one pause.
The crack is moving down the wall.
We must remain until the roof falls in.

2.

Men we once honored share a crooked eye.
We can do nothing more than mourn.
The girls we loved will marry them, and die.

Was it the age that they were ruined by?

Was there no prophet who could warn?
Men we once honored share a crooked eye.

Their wells are poisoned, choked with mud, or dry.
There is a weakness even in their scorn.
The girls we loved will marry them, and die.

There is a pattern to the way they cry,
Cursing the special hour they were born.
Men we once honored share a crooked eye.

They speak of honor, yet they lie:
All their certificates of truth are torn.
The girls we loved will marry them, and die.

Their promise fades like powder in the sky,
Their fanfares issue from a sour horn.
Men we once honored share a crooked eye;
The girls we loved will marry them, and die.

3. *A Villanelle for the Publisher Who Rejected* ——*'s Book*
Stiffen your features at anything new:
Of all the things you do, you do that best.
From your snug vantage point I scarcely like the view.

You have a way of saying, "True,
But what of readers in the West?"
Stiffen your features at anything new.

"Among the public," you will say, "so few
Would welcome just the attitude he's stressed."
From your snug vantage point I scarcely like the view.

"We're liberal here, we welcome every hue,

But not the strange, unfashionable, or the obsessed."
Stiffen your features at anything new.

"I turned down Joyce myself. It was the thing to do.
He, like so many these days, just befouled his nest."
From your snug vantage point I scarcely like the view.

So, for your services to all that's shoddy and untrue,
I gladly pin this dime-store medal on your chest.
Stiffen your features at anything new.
From your snug vantage point I scarcely like the view.

4.
No sound except the beating of a drum
Is heard along this walled-in corridor.
"Time will go by," we heard; "no messages will come."

The guests seem sad without their opium.
They stare at me and talk about the war.
There is no sound except the beating of a drum.

They want a different noise; like me, they thumb
Through heavy books we keep behind the door.
"Time will go by," we heard; "no messages will come."

Noise with complexity, however glum,
Might give some clue to what there is in store,
But there's no sound except the beating of a drum.

A few wear beards, or sleep all day, while some
Have grown quite philosophical. Some pace the floor.
"Time will go by," we heard; "no messages will come."

I think it is our hearts. Each paralyzed and numb
With waiting. Yet what is it we are waiting for?

No sound except the beating of a drum?
"Time will go by," we heard. "No messages will come."

5.
We had the notion it was dawn,
But it was only torches on the height.
The truce was signed, but the attack goes on.

The major fell down on the blackened lawn
And cried like a fool; his face was white.
We had the notion it was dawn.

On a bombed wall someone had drawn
A picture of a nude hermaphrodite.
The truce was signed, but the attack goes on.

Our food was rotten, all our water gone.
We had penicillin and dynamite,
And had the notion it was dawn

Because a cold gleam, fitful, gray, and wan,
Held for a moment in the signal's light.
The truce was signed, but the attack goes on.

We helped to choose these fields we crawl upon.
Sired in caskets, born to die at night,
We had the notion it was dawn.
The truce was signed, but the attack goes on.

A BRIEF INTRODUCTION
TO THE HISTORY OF CULTURE

*Such was the natural course of decay . . . Tasso bowed before
the mutilation; indeed, professed his readiness to make every
change demanded . . .*

"And if the name of 'Mage' offends these gentlemen,
It shall be 'Sage' instead. I've cut that queer enchanted wand,
Those cold blue foaming waters opening,
Although no bright Jerusalem was there.
My characters instead go underground through caves.
Let odors of black art float up from other manuscripts,
Not mine.
          "And I have cut the resurrection of the buried man,
The metamorphosis of warriors into creatures of the sea.
(Two Marys guide me to the Eucharist.)
The ship was marvelous, but it will have to go
As well; I multiply the orthodox. Those stanzas that conclude
A canto near the end—although examined, tolerated,
Almost, one might say, approved,
By the Inquisitor, I've doctored anyway.

"—Of course, the marvels must come out,
The kisses-stanza, and the parrot, too—
It seems a shame. Impediments at Rome,
Monsignor Silvio. I look toward Venice furtively.
Have I been over-theological?"

POEM INSTEAD OF A LETTER

Grasping at nothing in a swirl of leaves
Here in this smoky-faced and ruined town,
I think of you, across the continent,
Testing your smile that ripened in catasrophe
And wonderfully ready now for death.

The threadbare promise of our heritage
Is habit now; that other year turned winter
As we watched the fragments of a world
Dropping to pieces like a sick bouquet,
Missing the odor, though we named the time
Sufficiently. We know that odor now,
I think, as well as it is safe to know.
And even as I climb the steps, wishing you luck,
It fills the porches and the streets, while this rank wind
Blows through your rooms, untenanted.

What ranker winds may blow one cannot say,
Nor guess. The one tonight blows through the mind,
And every syllable is false, and dry.
Goodnight, goodnight. To strangers, to an empty street.

THAT WINTER

Cold ground and colder stone
Unearthed in ruined passageways,
The parodies of buildings in the snow—
Snow tossed and raging through a world
It imitates, that drives forever north
To what is rumored to be Spring.

To see the faces you had thought were put away
Forever, swept like leaves among the crowd,
Is to be drawn like them, on winter afternoons,
To avenues you saw demolished years before.
The houses still remain like monuments,
Their windows cracked, For Sale signs on the lawns.

Then grass upon those lawns again!—and dogs
In fashion twenty years ago, the streets mysterious
Through summer shade, the marvelous worlds
Within the world, each opening like a hand
And promising a constant course.—You see yourself,
A fool with smiles, one you thought dead.
And snow is raging, raging, in a darker world.

ABSTRACTS OF DISSERTATIONS

Andrea indicated he was not the first
To doubt. In 1530 Bembo wrote a monograph.
The years went by. P. de la Rue
Rejected Virgil. Was this Frenchman's theory true?

Consider it. J. Hildebrandt believed
In a Virgilian nucleus. Skutsch added fuel
To the dispute; he mentioned Gallus' name.
He died. After a while the twentieth century came.

Which brought us Vollmer, arbitrary, blunt,
Who said, "Authentic." Frank and Drew agreed.
Mackail unmasked their subtle fallacies.
Was this the end? Was there no more to hunt?

The type swims, and one hurries past
Fairclough's criteria, the Ovid mystery,
And turns the page . . . New knee-jerk stimuli . . .
Results from upper-income states . . . *Evesthes hooveri* . . .

Playas are smooth mud plains that lie
In bolsons' bottoms, found in Northern Mexico . . .
The ammo aldehydes . . . "The Thought of Edward Smedley
   Roach". . .
"Mortality of Fish: A Rational Approach."

GIRL AT MIDNIGHT

Then walk the floor, or twist upon your bed
While bullets, cold and blind, rush backward from the target's
    eye,
And say, "I will not dream that dream again. I will not dream
Of long-spent whispers vanishing down corridors
That turn through buildings I have never known;
The snap of rubber gloves; the tall child, blind,
Who calls my name; the stained sheets
Of another girl. And then a low bell,
Sounding through shadows in the cold,
Disturbs the screen that is my mind in sleep.

"—Your face is never clear. You always stand
In charcoal doorways in the dark. Part of your face
Is gone. You say, 'Just to be through with this damned world.
Contagious fogs blow in. Christ, we could die
The way deer sometimes do, their antlers locked,
Rotting in snow.'
           "And I can never speak.
But have I ever told the truth to you?
I did not ask for this; a new disease threads in.
I want your lips upon my lips, your mouth
Upon my breasts, again, again, again, again;
I want the morning filled with sun.

"But I must dream once more of cities burned away,
Corrupted wood, and silence on the piers.
Love is a sickroom with the roof half gone
Where nights go down in a continual rain.

Heart, heart. I do not live. The lie of peace
Echoes to no end; the clocks are dead.
What we have had we will not have again."

CRIME CLUB

Nó butler, no second maid, no blood upon the stair.
No eccentric aunt, no gardener, no family friend
Smiling among the bric-a-brac and murder.
Only a suburban house with the front door open
And a dog barking at a squirrel, and the cars
Passing. The corpse quite dead. The wife in Florida.

Consider the clues: the potato masher in a vase,
The torn photograph of a Wesleyan basketball team,
Scattered with check stubs in the hall;
The unsent fan letter to Shirley Temple,
The Hoover button on the lapel of the deceased,
The note: "To be killed this way is quite all right with me."

Small wonder that the case remains unsolved,
Or that the sleuth, Le Roux, is now incurably insane,
And sits alone in a white room in a white gown,
Screaming that all the world is mad, that clues
Lead nowhere, or to walls so high their tops cannot be seen;
Screaming all day of war, screaming that nothing can be
    solved.

XANTHA STREET

I close my eyes and all I see is rain
And bruised mouths lined above the silverware.
But rooms are empty as the country now:
The angels rise to Heaven spendidly
On page 289, but the evening still comes on.

Poorly cast in an eighth-rate Grand Guignol
Where every agonist proclaims his purity,
One's sight grows sharper in the glass:
The climate of murder hastens newer weeds,
And crippled neighbors wear divergent frowns
That no one saw before.—Nailed up in a box,
Nailed up in a pen, nailed up in a room
That once enclosed you amiably, you write,
"Finished. No more. The end," signing your name,
Frantic, but proud of penmanship. Beasts howl outside;
Authorities, however, keep the pavements clean.

It is to them that every face is turned,
Who steady rooms this earthquake rocks,
Graphing some future, indistinct, already frayed.
These rooms of ours are those that rock the worst.
Cold in the heart and colder in the brain,
We blink in darkened rooms toward exits that are gone.

Part Three

A GOOD CHORD ON A BAD PIANO

The fissures in the studio grow large.
Transplantings from the Rivoli, no doubt.
Such latter-day disfigurements leave out
All mention of those older scars that merge
On any riddled surfaces about.

Disgusting to be sure. On days like these,
A good chord on a bad piano serves
As well as shimmering harp-runs for the nerves.
F minor, with the added sixth. The keys
Are like old yellow teeth; the pedal swerves;

The treble wires vibrate, break, and bend;
The padded mallets fly apart.
Both instrument and room have made a start.
Piano and scene are double to the end,
Like all the smashed-up baggage of the heart.

RIVER SONG

By the public hook for the private eye,
Near the neutral river where the children were,
I was hung for the street, to watch the sky.

When they strung me there, I waved like a flag
Near the bright blue river where the children played,
And my smile became part of the cultural lag.

I named three martyrs. My mother came
To the grayish river where the children stared:
"My son, you have honored the family name."

I was happy. Then a parade went by
Near the shadowy river where the children waved,
And the uniforms made me shiver and cry.

I tried to get down. What I had learned
Near the sunless river where the children screamed
Was only pain. My ropemarks burned.

But I couldn't move. Had I been thrown
By the darkening river where the children failed,
Or had I come there quite alone?

The bands were playing when they cut me down
By the dirty river where the children cried,
And a man made a speech in a long black gown.

He called me a hero. I didn't care.
The river ran blood and the children died.
And I wanted to die, but they left me there.

THE HEAT IN THE ROOM

A good night for the fireplace to be
Crackling with flames—or so he figured,
Crumpling the papers he could only see
As testimonials to long plateaus of emptiness.

Watching in silence, she tried listening to the storm,
And thought obscurely, "He is burning both of us.
He is burning up our lives." She would have gone
To him and touched his hand, except for fear.

The ragged trees in lightning, blacker than before,
Moved nearer to the room. "If only I could stop
The pounding of my heart," she thought, "I might—"
But his face, a tight orange mask that burned,

Was held as though he faced a looking glass
And saw another face behind his own.
The fire seemed about to die. Then suddenly the flames
Roared like a white-hot furnace, and she screamed.

THE BELL FROM EUROPE

The tower bell in the Tenth Street Church
Rang out nostalgia for the refugee
Who knew the source of bells by sound.
We liked it, but in ignorance.
One meets authorities on bells infrequently.

Europe alone made bells with such a tone,
Herr Mannheim said. The bell
Struck midnight, and it shook the room.
He had heard bells in Leipzig, Chartres, Berlin,
Paris, Vienna, Brussels, Rome.
He was a white-faced man with sad enormous eyes.

Reader, for me that bell marked nights
Of restless tossing in this narrow bed,
The quarrels, the slamming of a door,
The kind words, friends for drinks, the books we read,
Breakfasts with streets in rain.
It rang from Europe all the time.
That was what Mannheim said.

It is good to know, now that the bell strikes noon.
In this day's sun, the hedges are Episcopalian
As noon is marked by the twelve iron beats.
The rector moves ruminantly among the gravestones,
And the sound of a dead Europe hangs in the streets.

THE DOCTOR WILL RETURN

The surgical mask, the rubber teat
Are singed, give off an evil smell.
You seem to weep more now that heat
Spreads everywhere we look.
It says here none of us is well.

The warty spottings on the figurines
Are nothing you would care to claim.
You seem to weep more since the magazines
Began revivals on the Dundas book.
It says here you were most to blame.

But though I cannot believe that this is so,
I mark the doctor as a decent sort.
I mix your medicine and go
Downstairs to leave instructions for the cook.
It says here time is getting short.

That I can believe. I hear you crying in your room
While watching traffic, reconciled.
Out in the park, black flowers are in bloom.
I picked some once and pressed them in a book.
You used to look at them, and smile.

YEAR'S END

The state cracked where they left your breath
No longer instrument. Along the shore
The sand ripped up, and the newer blood
Streaked like a vein to every monument.
The empty smoke that drifted near the guns
Where the stiff motor pounded in the mud
Had the smell of a hundred burned-out suns.
The ceiling of your sky went dark.
A year ago today they cracked your bones.

So rot in a closet in the ground
For the bad trumpets and the capitol's
Long seasonable grief. Rot for its guests,
Alive, that step away from death. Yet you,
A year cold, come more living to this room
Than these intruders, vertical and warm.

DEATH UNDER GLASS

He found the hothouse hotter than he hoped
Hell or baked Florida might be for any enemy.
And so through hairy ferns and brick-red pottery he groped
His humid destination, while the green glass sunlight
Broke into squares and crossed him as he went.

We steam like clams here; but we may not hiss
Without some peril, puffing toward the roses.
And roses of a monstrous size; how could he miss
Them, even though the sweat was pouring down his eyes?
He passed a mossy fountain and went on.

The rooms became like tanks, the roof might see him swim
Enclosed with all such steaming endocarp and chlorophyll,
Which pollened jungle air can never dim.
But lights, lungs, liver of impatient man
Can drown. He dropped into a pool and could not breathe.

He tried again. Dead tired, man walking underwater,
Drenched and bewildered man, undone, who loathed all roses
Then turned back, though lips of mistress, wife, or daughter
Had cried for them, huge thornless roses. Going down,
He tore at the long weeds as one might tear a gown.

ROUTES TO HEADQUARTERS

The first, preaxial digit of the hind
Stubs back a little for a fresher start.
We move this way to keep from going blind.

In great dust storms like these, the punctured heart
Is hasty pudding shaken in a bag,
Which you could mold, effendi, with the art

You crowd together from your own unease—
Some mildewed plunder fit for cats to drag
Around the house, smashed congeries.

We limped too long, though, wanting you to stay.
Those storms grew normal as the noise of guns.
Our pulpy hearts leaked better every day.

We acted when you proved yourself a beast.
Saw clearly how to end your life, made plans
To ship ourselves in boxes to the East

Where we attained a bland maturity.
—Then the long coma, hearts annealed, to stare
With glassy eyeballs toward the churning sea.

Part Four

(*These thirteen poems from* The Last Man *were reprinted as Part Four of this later book:* Variations on a Theme by Joyce, Praise to the Mind, White Collar Ballad, For My Daughter, For H.V. (1901–1927), After the Trial, A Cornucopia for Daily Use, Aunt Elizabeth, Early Winter, To the North, Obituary, The View of the Castle, *and* The Smiles of the Bathers. *They are to be found in their original positions.*)

POEMS 1947-1954

. . . those dark caverns into which all
men must descend, if they would know
anything beneath the surface and
illusive pleasures of existence.
Hawthorne, *The Marble Faun*

To Sarah and John

Part One

THE HOURGLASS

1.

Not the long case maple clock, insistent in the hall
At teatime, or the sound of tower bells
Through ivy, wakefulness and moonlight,
Washed over the sleeping summer roofs
Of cities, or even Grandfather's old silver Waltham
That he did not leave you, ticking at the dark
In another house, or even a whistle at noon; not these,
But a shadow on a cave's wall, lengthening.

Watch: a state of watchfulness, or the act
Of watching. Divide the night into three of them,
Or four, or five, depending upon
Your role as Hebrew, Roman or Greek.
Change the crew at port and starboard. Mark
The face of the stone when the sun goes down.
And mark particularly your passing face against the glass.
For in the violent stream, a thing is observed
And carried away, and another comes in place,
And it too will be carried away. A plume of steam
Hisses above the factory, and a thousand
Ham sandwiches come out of the lunch pails.

2.

A series of dusks, gray,
Blown like chimney smoke
And edged with lavender,
Descend, foregathering.
Tonight's dusk, swept with fog
Across the empty bay,

Is suddenly alive with birds
That plunge in silence
Where the breakers end.
The evening wakens and begins
Along the shore's edge, spreading,
Shrouded. Squares of light
Glow on the hill
Under a cold star.

The crew is changed, the stone's face
Notched in darkness.

Cats rally at this hour. Leaves
And the wind among the leaves
Take on the furred enchantments of a mouse,
Sounds in the walls at night,
Or yarn drawn knowingly across the floor.
The three of them are wild
Among the bushes on the hill: black shapes
And gray shapes, rapt
Pursuers of a time of night.

But now another dusk,
Swept with the leaves,
Mingles and laces with the mist tonight.
It is twenty years ago.
A gooseneck lamp
Lowers its broken head
In a threadbare room
Where strangers spit out olive pits
And drink from thumb-smeared jars,
And a phonograph plays *Sweet Savannah Sue*.

The rug is like a palimpsest.
Each face is like a palimpsest,
Watching. A shadow
Slides. Another dusk,

Far, farther back, begins, enveloping
Two figures by a lake,
Who, turning from each other,
Face their separate dusks. Trapped,
They separate interminably, prepare
The scenes ahead: a gooseneck lamp,
The darkened bay, returning dusks like these,
White birds descending, and the cats,
Resourceful at a haunted time.

Real, True, Empty, Mathematical, Continuous,
Solar, Galilean, Reversible, Sidereal, Absolute,
Noumenal, Phenomenal. But when oil gets on the hairspring,
When the teeth of the hour-wheel catch
On a notch of the barrel cover, when vandals
Push over the base of the sundial, one is late
To the office, another arrives in the middle
Of Act II, the beagle is not fed
At his usual time. High in the tower
Of St. Mark's, the twelve-foot dial used to tell
The hours, months, and phases of the moon. Spangled
With golden stars and trimmed with lapis lazuli,
A gilt bronze one-ton lion closed its wings beneath.
Four times a day, three robot kings,
Preceded by an angel with
A golden trumpet, issued from a door
And bowed to a Madonna, vanishing

Behind another door.—A shadow slides
Against the cave's wall. Hidden on a roof
Above slow traffic in a failing light,
I watched the owls march, in solemn file,
Past monuments, intent against the dusk and time,
Deserting the metropolis, and wished them well.

And saw a shadow spread across the city, lengthening.

Hunched by the sill, I stare
At ghosts, resourcelessly,
Except, perhaps, the resource of
The ghosts themselves,
Familiar, certain, and perhaps desired,
At fog that rises on the hill,
Hearing again, somewhere above the roof,
The sound of time, the sounds of nightfall.

3.
Being at the expense of Becoming.
Becoming at the expense of Being.
The statue's head falls off, suggesting
That ideal forms may be non-temporal.
Tide covers the sand.

What transcends Becoming
Can never be reached by Becoming.
Regard the higher and higher forms
Continually perfecting themselves.
Under the door, dust, and the north wind.

Becoming infests all time with instability
And imperfection, yet only in this way

Is Being shifted and transformed.
Once out of time and your chance is gone.
Here, in the rubble, clear a passageway.

4.
Where dust had blown,
I walked a track
Through brittle weeds.
The sky leaned, overcast,
And dead seeds
Chattered at my back.
I was in the past
Somewhere, alone.

My mind shaped routes
For some immense retreat
Out of the world of men,
When suddenly I saw my feet
In hiking boots
That I had worn when I was ten
Years old. My beard was gone.
And I was on a street
Of wooden bungalows,
Block after block,
Where I had been before.
The air grew cold and still.
And in the shade
Before my father's house
I waited on the walk, afraid,
And heard, through an opening door,
Immense and terrible,
The ticking of a clock.

5.

The crew is changed, the stone's face notched in darkness.

Held in the rouged and marketable glow
Beyond Third Avenue, the city hums
Like muffled bees. Sheeted, we lie
Above the streets, where headlights
Search the mirrors through the heat
And move on, reverential over the cement.
—Sleep. But there is no sleep. Far down on Lexington,
A siren moans and dies. A drunk is sobbing
In the hall. Upstairs, an organ record
Of a Baptist hymn comes on. Past one o'clock.
It is the time of seconal, of loss, of
Heartbeats of a clock, enormous, by your bed,
Of noises in the walls,
Of one more drink.—A shadow slides.
Drawn toward the window, I look down like one
Who sees his life spread out upon the pavements
And finds a death renewed. Here, for a time,
I lived, to circumscribe and praise
Such residue of splendor as remained
In the soft mornings and the glow of rooms
At nightfall, ardent with music and the speech of friends,
Knowing, through all that harbored time, the light was lessen-
    ing.

Now from a corner of the street there comes
A sound like old seeds shaken in a gourd,
Where ghosts take up their wanderings
On routes the owls improvised. A shadow
Slides. And the past instant, charged with loss,

A speck in time, secured, sustained
Between the future and the past
By space—by headlights and the haunted streets—
Endures and is not lost. In Prague,
Above the City Hall, Death's figure stands
Against the dial of a calendar, and sounds a bell
Before the hour strikes. The scythe-man cuts
The old in two, a woodcut on a yellowed page,
Preparing for the young, who will arrive
To find the city marbled with desire. Time
Mows the brittle stalks of autumn as
It stirs the fresh grass, heals all things
And shapes the blood of new wounds. Shadows slide.
The squirrel turns in his cage, shale
Tumbles from a mountain to a road,
A planet surges, plunging, and goes out.

THE LIVES

"History is a grave and noble pageant," Landor said.
His family life at Gherardesca proved impossible.
In 1844 his daughter gave him Pomero, a dog.

The pictures blacken in their frames, the tassels on the bed-
 spread
Fall. "He laughs like an ogre," Mrs. Browning said,
Who did not relish him the way her husband did.

Stuffed animals and birds, antiques of plaster gave
A tone to Boston. Santayana, who had stomach trouble
As a youth, once shook the hand

Of Henry Wadsworth Longfellow. Professor Norton
Lingered on. "No comfort, not a breath of love,"
Wrote Nietzsche, going mad. Booth Tarkington loved art.

"Well, history is a grave and noble pageant," Landor said.
"Or 'stately pageant' is perhaps the term."

On the neglected lawn, the iron dogs and the deer,
Rusted among the weeds, alert, indomitable, keep watch.

THE TESTIMONY OF JAMES APTHORP

1.

A wall. A chair. A bed. A chiffonier.
Ice fills the vacant places of the street.
Not yet with silica or cinnabar
Will I be healed. Not yet—my hair
Scraped, bearded, to the skull—
With parsley out of Macedonia. (The druggist
Shuffled toward me in a dirty coat. I did not like
The way he grinned, the way the vaseline and aspergum
Were spread. "We do not carry that," he said. A jar was there
Among the hairnets.) Now I hear the ice
Filling the vacant places, frozen. Blackened seeds
Drop from the peony; and once again
The hinges of the heart creak open on
A season echoed with iniquity,
Predictable, and almost welcome now. The autumn
Came, and then a winter. I hugged the wall
Along the lake. Under the freezing sun,
Where once my throat, along with summer, bled,
I traced your name down to a deeper ice,
My hair scraped, bearded, to the skull.

2.

It was a room like any other. On the sill,
A rhododendron in a jar. In sepia,
Framed on the wall, a photograph
Of Rheims, where figures walked,
Or seemed to walk, in lamplight. Falling asleep,
Toward dusk, I'd wake to see them walking,

Upside down. And I kept walking, too.
Over the foxtails and the drying tar,
Sparse grass and brownish weeds, the washed-up rafts
And timbers on the beach . . . A bed. A lamp.
A wall. A chair. A chiffonier. Now,
At a distance, hills, where no one walks.
The vacant places fill with ice.
I think of how the pygmies used to climb,
Sliding in sand, then climbed again,
Falling, and how the clouds
Came over in the heat. I used to see
Them, just behind my eyes, before
Dusk came, and with it, usually,
The lights attending, and a kind of sleep.

3.

One of them floated downstream all night in the cold,
After the long jump from the bridge; another, bleeding,
Dying in a ditch near Randall's Creek, the paper said—
A girl of eight, with cancer, sick
For months and newly dusted with the snow.
I used to walk there. Now the vacant places
Fill with ice, and break. They found
Her older sister trying on her clothes at home; her mother
At a bar on Xantha Street. She had the axe.—I hugged the wall
Along the lake. The tar had dried. He moved along the counter,
Toward me, in a dirty coat. They all float downstream now.
—And then it freezes and the edge of things is still.

4.

I could not mean to kill
A druggist at a store. But seeds,
Black and predictable, fall from the peonies
And tick along the hardwood floor, like beads. Sparse grass
Grows through the cracks. That isn't Rheims. Rheims cracks
    apart.
Why don't they all give up and give it to you straight
And say they can't heal anything? Those shrines
Where cripples dump their trusses and their canes—
Throw me there, too, against the crutches;
Let me die. Not silica, not cinnabar,
Not parsley out of Macedonia. I did not mean to kill
The druggist at the store. I felt the ice
That cracked as Rheims went down. A wall.
A chair. A chiffonier.—I broke his head in
With a jar of facial blemish cream. He kept on grinning,
Going down. So many hairnets, all those salves,
And how they used to climb, and we can't even climb,
Falling, gone downhill, pushed against the rafts,
Smeared on the foxtails and the tar, screaming,
Screaming and walking, upside down,
While ice fills up the world.

ROUND

"Wondrous life!" cried Marvell at Appleton House.
Renan admired Jesus Christ "wholeheartedly."
But here dried ferns keep falling to the floor,
And something inside my head
Flaps like a worn-out blind. Royal Cortissoz is dead.
A blow to the *Herald-Tribune.* A closet mouse
Rattles the wrapper on the breakfast food. Renan
Admired Jesus Christ "wholeheartedly."

Flaps like a worn-out blind. Cézanne
Would break out in the quiet streets of Aix
And shout, "Le monde, c'est terrible!" Royal
Cortissoz is dead. And something inside my head
Flaps like a worn-out blind. The soil
In which the ferns are dying needs more Vigoro.
There is no twilight on the moon, no mist or rain,
No hail or snow, no life. Here in this house

Dried ferns keep falling to the floor, a mouse
Rattles the wrapper on the breakfast food. Cézanne
Would break out in the quiet streets and scream. Renan
Admired Jesus Christ "wholeheartedly." And something in-
    side my head
Flaps like a worn-out blind. Royal Cortissoz is dead.
There is no twilight on the moon, no hail or snow.
One notes fresh desecrations of the portico.
"Wondrous life!" cried Marvell at Appleton House.

100

TURTLE

To William Baziotes

Watching, beside the road,
A turtle crawl (with smells
Of autumn closing in,
Night traffic roaring by),

I felt a husk that moved
Inside me, torpid, dry
As air from a long-closed room
That drifts through an opening door

When the wind in the hall is right—
Moved as a turtle moves
Into the covering grass,
Far in the woods, at night.

A PASTICHE FOR EVE

Unmanageable as history: these
Followers of Tammuz to the land
That offered no return, where dust
Grew thick on every bolt and door. And so the world
Chilled, and the women wept, tore at their hair.
Yet, in the skies, a goddess governed Sirius, the Dog,
Who shines alike on mothers, lesbians, and whores.

What are we governed by? Dido and Carrie
Chapman Catt arrange themselves as statues near
The playground and the Tivoli. While warming up the beans,
Miss Sanders broods on the Rhamnusian, the whole earth wor-
   shipping
Her godhead. Later, vegetables in Athens.
Chaste in the dungeon, swooning with voluptuousness,
The Lady of the Castle weds pure Christ, the feudal groom.

Their bowels almost drove Swift mad. "Sad stem,
Sweet evil, stretching out a lion's jaws," wrote Marbode.
Now we cling together in our caves. That not impossible she
That rots and wrinkles in the sun, the shadow
Of all men, man's counterpart, sweet rois
Of vertew and of gentilness . . . The brothel and the crib en-
   dure.
Past reason hunted. How we die! Their pain, their blood, are
   ours.

RETURN OF THE GHOST

No sudden leavetaking, by your grace,
This time, old ghost, so long abroad. Friend of this house,
Warm all your evanescence by this fire
That burns the both of us for ending nights.
All through my germinating years, you, unfatigued,
Obsessed the attic's dust, the cellar's dark,
Moaning belowstairs, creaking the doors.
The days marched with your continuities.

And now the nights begin. Your absence breeds
A longer silence through the rooms. We haunt ourselves.
There is a shutter, pounding in the mind,
Old spiderwebs that drift behind the eyes,
A moaning in the heart that warns insistently.
—Old ghost, friend of this house, remain!
What is there now to prod us toward
The past, our ruinous nostalgias?

1926

The porchlight coming on again,
Early November, the dead leaves
Raked in piles, the wicker swing
Creaking. Across the lots
A phonograph is playing *Ja-Da*.

An orange moon. I see the lives
Of neighbors, mapped and marred
Like all the wars ahead, and R.
Insane, B. with his throat cut,
Fifteen years from now, in Omaha.

I did not know them then.
My airedale scratches at the door.
And I am back from seeing Milton Sills
And Doris Kenyon. Twelve years old.
The porchlight coming on again.

THE UPSTAIRS ROOM

It must have been in March the rug wore through.
Now the day passes and I stare
At warped pine boards my father's father nailed,
At the twisted grain. Exposed, where emptiness allows,
Are the wormholes of eighty years; four generations' shoes
Stumble and scrape and fall
To the floor my father stained,
The new blood streaming from his head. The drift
Of autumn fires and a century's cigars, that gun's
Magnanimous and brutal smoke, endure.
In March the rug was ragged as the past. The thread
Rots like the lives we fasten on. Now it is August,
And the floor is blank, worn smooth,
And, for my life, imperishable.

GUIDE TO THE SYMPHONY

To Bob Helm

Three flutes, two oboes, English horn, violins,
Two clarinets, snare, tuba, tambourine,
And a contra-bassoon played by a worn-looking blonde.

The work is classical in form. *Mit Kraft:*
A wayward dance proceeds; the woodwind voices and the strings
Unite in *agitato* passages that state,

Some critics believe, "Man's long revolt against the Higher Will."
Staccato notes, *fortissimo,* engage the clarinets.
The work is dissonant, "though not excessively."

An agitated, almost angry theme ensues, in F.
(Trombones.) A struggle. (Flutes.) And then the scherzo movement,
Lachrymose, so often thought to deal

With Western Man's religious hopes gone dim.
Drums; and the famous "Wailing of the Damned" motif.
(Bassoons.)
A horn sounds yearningly. A short ejaculation from the fifes.

Man's nature sweetens (key of B flat); and the reeds,
Augmented by an alto sax, pick up
A hopeful theme (*allegro moderato*), though

Baumgarten writes that Koussevitsky used instead
A *moderato* beat.—But now the gloom
Has deepened once again; the heckelphone implores

In 2/4 time, the cellos. Morning. Pan awakes.
Sunrise. Entrance of the false Messiahs. Here
A surging countertheme, in E flat minor, and the oboes shrill.

The specter of a dead waltz drifts
In sleep. Bass flutes, violas, and the English horn
Repeat the second theme, in fifths. Sad

Pizzicati of the strings. A bell sounds, and the violins
Lash furiously, subside, diminishing.
(All this in E flat major.) Clarinets sing plaintively.

The last stroke of the hammer. (Tympani.) The sacred stag
Is dead. Long anguished *tuttis* by the brass. A final roll of
    drums.
It ends. The concertmaster rubs a little resin on his bow.

LAND'S END

A day all blue and white, and we
Came out of woods to sand
And snow-capped waves. The sea
Rose with us as we walked, the land
Built dunes, a lighthouse, and a sky of gulls.

Here where I built my life ten years ago,
The day breaks gray and cold;
And brown surf, muddying the shore,
Deposits fish-heads, sewage, rusted tin.
Children and men break bottles on the stones.
Beyond the lighthouse, black against the sky,
Two gulls are circling where the woods begin.

SARATOGA ENDING

1.

Iron, sulphur, steam: the wastes
Of all resorts like this have left their traces.
Old canes and crutches line the walls. Light
Floods the room, stripped from the pool, broken
And shimmering like scales. Hidden
By curtains, women dry themselves
Before the fire and review
The service at hotels,
The ways of dying, ways of sleep,
The blind ataxia patient from New York,
And all the others who were here a year ago.

2.

Visconti, mad with pain. Each day,
Two hundred drops of laudanum. Hagen, who writhes
With every step. The Count, a shrunken penis
And a monocle, dreaming of horses in the sun,
Covered with flies.—Last night I woke in sweat
To see my hands, white, curled upon the sheet
Like withered leaves. I thought of days
So many years ago, hauling driftwood up from the shore,
Waking at noon, the harbor birds following
Boats from the mainland. And then no thoughts at all.
Morphine at five. A cold dawn breaking. Rain.

3.

I lie here in the dark, trying to remember
What my life has taught me. The driveway lights blur
In the rain. A rubber-tired metal cart goes by,
Followed by a nurse; and something rattles
Like glasses being removed after

A party is over and the guests have gone.
Test tubes, beakers, graduates, thermometers—
Companions of these years that I no longer count.
I reach for a cigarette and my fingers
Touch a tongue depressor that I use
As a bookmark; and all I know
Is the touch of this wood in the darkness, remembering
The warmth of one bright summer half a life ago—
A blue sky and a blinding sun, the face
Of one long dead who, high above the shore,
Looked down on waves across the sand, on rows of yellow jars
In which the lemon trees were ripening.

DOG

To Vincent Hugh

"This night is monstrous winter when the rats
Swarm in great packs along the waterfront,
When midnight closes in and takes away your name.
And it was Rover, Ginger, Laddie, Prince;
My pleasure hambones. Donned a collar once
With golden spikes, the darling of a cultured home
Somewhere between the harbor and the heights, uptown.
Or is this something curs with lathered mouths invent?
They had a little boy I would have bitten, had I dared.
They threw great bones out on the balcony.
But where? I pant at every door tonight.

I knew this city once the way I know those lights
Blinking in chains along the other side,
These streets that hold the odors of my kind.
But now, my bark a ghost in this strange scentless air,
I am no growling cicerone or cerberus
But wreckage for the pound, snuffling in shame
All cold-nosed toward identity.—Rex? Ginger? No.
A sort of panic jabbering inside begins.
Wild for my shadow in this vacantness,
I can at least run howling toward the bankrupt lights
Into the traffic where bones, cats, and masters swarm.
And where my name must be."

TESTIMONIES

"Others at their porches . . ."

1.
"I baited bears and prayed. The Queen
Grew inky on Boethius. Between
The angels and the animals we lived and died.
The sun, the King, and my own being blazed as one.
I spoke occasionally to God."

2.
"I circumcise my son and laud
The covenant. The massacres go on.
And now, plunder, expulsion. Poisoned fountains drown
The Synagogue. Blood stains the font;
The staff breaks toward the desert in my hands."

3.
"I did not see the Grail. Sir John
Lay dying at the bridge. When barbers cut away
Those spongy growths from the poor soldiers' gums,
The whole camp echoed with our cries.
I place the cauldron of God's wrath upon the coals."

4.
"I watch the world contract to this
Gray winter Grub Street where the scavengers
Drop in the cold. The famine spreads more every day.
God save the King, the Army, and the House of Lords!
The rags fall from my arms outside the coffee-house."

5.
"I live. The Elevated shudders to a stop
At Twenty-Eighth and Third. Among
The nuns and crippled Negroes, we descend
The stairway to the street, to red-cheeked chromo Christ,
Hung with the bloody calves' heads in the butcher shop."

TRAVELS IN NORTH AMERICA

To Lorraine and Robert Wilbur

Here is San Luis Obispo. Here
Is Kansas City, and here is Rovere,
Kentucky. And here, a small black dot,
Unpronounceable but hard to forget,
Is where we stopped at the Seraphim Motel,
And well-fed moths flew out to greet us from the walls
On which a dado of petunias grew.
We threw a nickel in the wishing well,
But the moths remained, and the petunias too.

And here is Santa Barbara where
They had the heated swimming pool.
Warm in our room, we watched the bathers' breaths. My hair
Fell out in Santa Barbara, and the cold
Came blowing off the sea. An ancient gull
Dropped down to shiver gravely in the steady rain.
The sea-food dinner Duncan Hines had praised
Gave off a classic taste of tin. The weather was unseasonable.
There was a landmark, I remember, that was closed.

Here is the highway in and out of Cincinnati.
An inch or so of line along the river. Driving west
One Sunday in a smoky dawn, burnt orange along the land-
    scape's rim,
The radio gave forth five solid and remembered hours
Of gospel singers and New Orleans jazz,
With terse, well-phrased commercials for a funeral home.
They faded out—Cleves, Covington, North Bend

114

Made way for Evansville and Patti Page. The roads end
At motels. The one that night had an Utrillo in a velvet
    frame.

The stars near Santa Fe are blurred and old, discolored
By a milky haze; a ragged moon
Near Albuquerque shimmers the heat. Autumnal light
Falls softly on a file of candy skulls
And metal masks. Sand drifts at noon, at nine,
And now at midnight on a Navajo in levis reading
Sartre in an Avon Pocket Book, against the window
Of a Rexall store. Here one descends
To shelvings of the pit. The valleys hollow out.

The land is terraced near Los Alamos: scrub cedars,
Piñon pines and ruined pueblos, where a line
Of tall young men in uniform keep watch upon
The University of California's atom bomb.
The sky is soiled and charitable
Behind barbed wire and the peaks of mountains—
Sangre de Christo, Blood of Christ, this "fitting portent
For the Capital of the Atomic Age." We meant
To stop, but one can only see so much. A mist
Came over us outside Tryuonyi: caves, and a shattered cliff.

And possibly the towns one never sees are best,
Preserved, remote, and merely names and distances.
Cadiz, Kentucky, "noted for the quality of hams it ships,
The home of wealthy planters," Dalton, Georgia,
"Center of a thriving bedspread industry, where rainbow lines
Of counterpanes may be observed along the highway. Here
The man whose *Home, Sweet Home* is known to all,

The champion of the Cherokee, John Howard Payne, was
tried."
—Wetumka, Oklahoma; Kipling, Michigan;

Glenrock, Wyoming; and Chehalis, Washington
Are momentarily the shifting centers of a dream,
Swept bare of formica and television aerials
And rows of cars that look a little more like fish each year.
—A dream that ends with towns that smell of rubber smould-
ering;
A brownish film sticks to the windshields
And the lungs; the skies are raining soot
And other specks that failed to fit into the paint
Or the salami. A cloud of grit sweeps over you and down the
street.

And sometimes, shivering in St. Paul or baking in Atlanta,
The sudden sense that you have seen it all before:
The man who took your ticket at the Gem in Council Bluffs
Performed a similar function for you at the Shreveport Tivoli.
Joe's Lunch appears again, town after town, next door
To Larry's Shoe Repair, adjoining, inescapably, the Acme
Doughnut Shop.
Main, First, and Market fuse together.
Bert and Lena run the laundromat. John Foster, D.D.S.,
Has offices above the City Bank.—At three or four,
On winter afternoons, when school is letting out
And rows of children pass you, near the firehouse,
This sense is keenest, piercing as the wind
That sweeps you toward the frosted door of your hotel
And past the portly hatted traveler with moist cigar
Who turns his paper as you brush against the rubber plant.

116

You have forgotten singularities. You have forgotten
Rooms that overlooked a park in Boston, brown walls hung

With congo masks and Mirós, rain
Against a skylight, and the screaming girl
Who threw a cocktail shaker at a man in tweeds
Who quoted passages from Marlowe and *'Tis Pity She's a
    Whore.*
You have forgotten yellow lights of San Francisco coming on,
The bridges choked with cars, and islands in the fog.
Or have forgotten why you left or why you came to where you
    are,
Or by what roads and passages,
Or what it was, if anything, that you were hoping for.

Journeys are ways of marking out a distance,
Or dealing with the past, however ineffectually,
Or ways of searching for some new enclosure in this space
Between the oceans.—Now the smaller waves of afternoon re-
    trace
This sand where breakers threw their cargoes up—
Old rafts and spongy two-by-fours and inner tubes,
The spines of sharks and broken codheads,
Tinned stuff with the labels gone, and yellow weeds
Like entrails; mattresses and stones, and, by a grapefruit crate,
A ragged map, imperfectly enclosed by seaworn oilskin.
Two tiny scarlet crabs run out as I unfold it on the beach.
Here, sodden, fading, green ink blending into blue,
Is Brooklyn Heights, and I am walking toward the subway
In a January snow again, at night, ten years ago. Here is
    Milpitas,
Calfornia, filling stations and a Ford

Assembly plant. Here are the washboard roads
Of Wellfleet, on the Cape, and summer light and dust.
And here, now textured like a blotter, like the going years
And difficult to see, is where you are, and where I am,
And where the oceans cover us.

Part Two

LA VITA NUOVA

Last summer, in the blue heat,
Over the beach, in the burning air,
A legless beggar lurched on calloused fists
To where I waited with the sun-dazed birds.
He said, "The summer boils away. My life
Joins to another life; this parched skin
Dries and dies and flakes away,
Becomes your costume when the torn leaves blow."

—Thus in the losing autumn,
Over the streets, I now lurch
Legless to your side and speak your name
Under a gray sky ripped apart
By thunder and the changing wind.

BACK

Much cry and little wool:
I have come back
As empty-handed as I went.

Although the woods were full,
And past the track
The heavy boughs were bent

Down to my knees with fruit
Ripe for a still life, I had meant
My trip as a search for stones.

But the beach was bare
Except for the drying bones
Of a fish, shells, an old wool

Shirt, a rubber boot,
A strip of lemon rind.
They were not what I had in mind:

It was merely stones.
Well, the days are full.
This day at least is spent.

Much cry and little wool:
I have come back
As empty-handed as I went.

DEAD MARCH

Under the bunker, where the reek of kerosene
Prepared the marriage rite, leader and whore,
Imperfect kindling even in this wind, burn on.

Someone in uniform hums Brahms. Servants prepare
Eyewitness stories as the night comes down, as smoking coals
    await
Boots on the stone, the occupying troops. Howl ministers.

Deep in Kyffhauser Mountain's underground,
The Holy Roman Emperor snores on, in sleep enduring
Seven centuries. His long red beard

Grows through the table to the floor. He moves a little.
Far in the labyrinth, low thunder rumbles and dies out.
Twitch and lie still. Is Hitler now in the Himalayas?

We are in Cleveland, or Sioux Falls. The architecture
Seems like Omaha, the air pumped in from Düsseldorf.
Cold rain keeps dripping just outside the bars. The testicles

Burst on the table as the commissar
Untwists the vise, removes his gloves, puts down
Izvestia. (Old saboteurs, controlled by Trotsky's

Scheming and unconquered ghost, still threaten Novgorod.)
—And not far from the pits, these bones of ours,
Burned, bleached, and splintering, are shoveled, ready for the
    fields.

THE LOCUSTS, THE PLAZA, THE ROOM

The wings fold fanwise and then snap like knives.
Beyond the mountains, clouds of locusts rose, sucked into the
    West,
While little dogs danced in the streets and strangely moaned.
Another cloud was funneled smoke against the sun.

I used to watch all this.

Atrocities outside the plaza, something about a stain
Somebody saw, reports of scuffles on a stair
Somebody interrupted, evidence of sabotage
In the orifice of a sponge. The Japanese, perhaps.

I used to believe all this.

You woke me when they turned the streetlights off.
Then new lights raced across the wall from windows to the
    door.
We made love while the bombers roared on by,
Gone seaward. The room rocked and the world closed in your
    eyes.

I used to know all this.

And now the plaza drenched in rain, the locusts
Gone, and eaten stems against the sky. And you, you,
Dead with the rest.—What have they done to me, what have I
Done to myself, entranced these days by only surfaces
Of worn and curious stones, the wet leaves shivering?

And now I live like this.

WEATHER FOR PILGRIMS

To William Poster

At the end of Thanksgiving Day,
Driving across the bridge
(The longest bridge in the world),
The old car rattled and groaned,
Choked and clattered and died.
Out of the rear the sludge
Poured joyously free, unfurled,
At the end of Thanksgiving Day.

The bearings were castanets
That knocked like the shattered gates
Guarding the points of the world,
Oozed like the eggs of a carp
At the end of Thanksgiving Day,
Bounced on the trafficked stone.
Oil poured over the hood
And the Chevrolets swam home

To turkeys stuffed with squares
Cellophaned-bagged and brown,
Celery and pumpkin pie,
Uncles too drunk to care,
Constipated but spry
At the end of Thanksgiving Day.
We dined on different fare,
Chewing the smog and spray

As flames spread up from the bands
And the glistening boats below

Sailed on to the Orient.
Upholstery smoked and glowed
As we warmed our thankful hands
At the end of Thanksgiving Day,
Knowing that hands are wise,
And praised the firm cement,
While turkeys flew down like flies
To roost and roast in the flames.

INTERREGNUM

Butcher the evil millionaire, peasant,
And leave him stinking in the square.
Torture the chancellor. Leave the ambassador
Strung by his thumbs from the pleasant
Embassy wall, where the vines were.
Then drill your hogs and sons for another war.

Fire on the screaming crowd, ambassador,
Sick chancellor, brave millionaire,
And name them by the name that is your name.
Give privilege to the wound, and maim
The last resister. Poison the air
And mew for peace, for order, and for war.

View with alarm, participant, observer,
Buried in medals from the time before.
Whisper, then believe and serve and die
And drape fresh bunting on the hemisphere
From here to India. This is the world you buy
When the wind blows fresh for war.

Hide in the dark alone, objector;
Ask a grenade what you are living for,
Or drink this knowledge from the mud.
To an abyss more terrible than war
Descend and tunnel toward a barrier
Away from anything that moves with blood.

PROBLEMS OF A JOURNALIST

"I want to get away somewhere and re-read Proust,"
Said an editor of *Fortune* to a man on *Time*.
But the fire roared and died, the phoenix quacked like a
    goose,
And all roads to the country fray like shawls
Outside the dusk of suburbs. Pacing the halls
Where mile-high windows frame a dream with witnesses,
You taste, fantast and epicure, the names of towns along the
    coast,
Black roadsters throbbing on the highways blue with rain
Toward one lamp, burning on those sentences.

"I want to get away somewhere and re-read Proust,"
Said an editor of *Newsweek* to a man on *Look*.
Dachaus with telephones, Siberias with bonuses.
One reads, as winter settles on the town,
The evening paper, in an Irving Place café.

A LATE HISTORY

To Herbert Cahoon

1.

Black, under the candlesticks, moving in harness
To a slow music, we hang the sepulchre
And hear the herald angels sing, "He is not here."
It is mid-November. The first snows
Have fallen silently over the town. I eat
Black pudding at the altar while a dove
Descends from the flaming tower. Later,
Dr. Rashdall, behind whose scholarship
A generation's knowledge burns, will unmask
Newman. But now it is mid-November.
I eat black pudding and the dove descends.

2.

In a hollow tree by the bridge, an owl awaits.
The moon is full and white. The stars are out.
Tall elms surround the statue of a nymph
Where old Etonians, festive in Norfolk jackets,
Commemorate D. G. Rossetti with a plaque.
I relish the scene, remembering old Watts-Dunton
Boasting, "Dogs have never bitten me!" that day
We talked about Rossetti. Later, attacks of gout,
That horrible baby that looked like Gosse, a wheelchair
Wobbling on toward Trinity, webs covering my eyes.
But tonight the moon is full, and white. Thus 1904 begins.

3.

Of the far end of Marseilles and the islands:
A dwarf climbing where the waves are luminous
With phosphorescent lights, where foam bursts into flower,
And the slow rise and fall of the ocean
Rocks the world. Moving like a crab over the sand,
He murmurs, "We can never praise the beauty of
The world enough, my friend." Later, death by starvation;
Until the end, swinging on a trapeze for an hour
Every day, longing to be tall. He left
Some wonderful paintings. I walk beside him now
At the far end of Marseilles, toward the islands.

4.

Now, now, if ever, love opening your eyes,
The great blind windows lifted toward the sun, the doors
Thrown open wide. I said to my heart,
Do I wake or sleep?—Soon, soon, these closings start
Where mornings held the garden captive; and early dusk,
Laden with mist and smoke, drifts upward from the grass.
The wind dies. The scraping leaves are still. I said to my
  heart,
Ravaged by darkness, "Now, Soon, and Later have become
Each other—doors all closed, the windows blocked and barred
  for good—
And all sink down together to the bottom of the sea.
Do I wake or sleep? It is as late tonight as it will ever be."

ASPECTS OF ROBINSON

Robinson at cards at the Algonquin; a thin
Blue light comes down once more outside the blinds.
Gray men in overcoats are ghosts blown past the door.
The taxis streak the avenues with yellow, orange, and red.
This is Grand Central, Mr. Robinson.

Robinson on a roof above the Heights; the boats
Mourn like the lost. Water is slate, far down.
Through sounds of ice cubes dropped in glass, an osteopath,
Dressed for the links, describes an old Intourist tour.
—Here's where old Gibbons jumped from, Robinson.

Robinson walking in the Park, admiring the elephant.
Robinson buying the *Tribune,* Robinson buying the *Times.* Robinson
Saying, "Hello. Yes, this is Robinson. Sunday
At five? I'd love to. Pretty well. And you?"
Robinson alone at Longchamps, staring at the wall.

Robinson afraid, drunk, sobbing Robinson
In bed with a Mrs. Morse. Robinson at home;
Decisions: Toynbee or luminol? Where the sun
Shines, Robinson in flowered trunks, eyes toward
The breakers. Where the night ends, Robinson in East Side
bars.

Robinson in Glen plaid jacket, Scotch-grain shoes,
Black four-in-hand and oxford button-down,
The jeweled and silent watch that winds itself, the brief-
Case, covert topcoat, clothes for spring, all covering
His sad and usual heart, dry as a winter leaf.

THE CLINIC

To Gregory Bateson

Light in the cage like burning foil
At noon; and I am caught
With all the other cats that howl
And dance and spit, lashing their tails
When the doctors turn the current on.
The ceiling fries. Waves shimmer from the floor
Where hell spreads thin between the bars.
And then a switch snaps off and it is over
For another day. Close up. Go home.
Calcium chloride, a milligram
Or so, needled into the brain, close to
The infundibulum. Sometimes we sleep for weeks.

                                                      Report
From Doctor Edwards: sixteen tests (five women, fourteen
    men).
Results are far from positive. Static ataxia,
Blood pressure, tapping, visual acuity. A Mrs. Wax
Could not recall a long ride in a Chevrolet
From Jersey to her home in Forest Hills. Fatigue
Reported by a few. These smoky nights
My eyes feel dry and raw; I tire
After twenty hours without sleep. Performance
At a lower ebb.—The lights
Have flickered and gone out.
There is a sound like winter in the streets.

                                                Vide Master,
Muzie, Brown and Parker on the hypoplastic heart.

Culpin stressed the psychogenic origin. DaCosta
Ruled out syphilis. If we follow Raines and Kolb,
We follow Raines and Kolb.—It's only a sort of wound,
From one of the wars, that opens up occasionally.
Signs of desiccation, but very little pain.

I followed Raines and Kolb, in that dark backward,
Seeking a clue; yet in that blackness, hardly a drop
Of blood within me did not shudder. Mouths without hands,
Eyes without light, my tongue dry, intolerable
Thirst. And then we came into that room
Where a world of cats danced, spat, and howled
Upon a burning plate.—And I was home.

SPEECHES AND LYRIC FOR A PLAY

A BROOKLYN MEDIUM PREPARES FOR A SEANCE:
Moles crawling from their hills
These damp and foggy nights
Blink toward the lights
Of far-off towns. They see
A blur of walls,
Stars, weeds in the wind,
Cars turning on a bend
In the beginning rain. Sometimes,
Like them, on all fours,
Crawling from my hole,
I look out at a world of doors
And silences, the glazed
Shapes drifting past like men,
And am apprehensive, dazed
That it still goes on—
Blinking, half-blind,
Toward a strange sun,
Hunched like a mole,
Needing the dark again.

CHORUS IN DARKNESS:
Geiger counter, clicking soon
In the forests of our noon,
What immortal eye will glimpse
These corpses, and our impotence?

SONG FOR A CHORUS OF SUBWAY RIDERS DESCENDING
    INTO THE TIMES SQUARE STATION OF THE IRT:
So walk through rain and drop into this hell

Where steam is rising and a bell
Rings like a phone. Once I was cut
Here, by a maniac, from ear to mouth.
One enters cautiously, alone.

Old Negresses, Wall Streeters, men
With eyes like knives. When
Will we live again? The doors slam shut.
The train roars south
Under water and stone.

TWO CHILDREN, RUMMAGING IN THE DEBRIS OF A
   DESTROYED BUILDING, DISCOVER THE FOLLOWING
   FRAGMENT OF A LETTER. ONE READS IT ALOUD:
My dear, now it is all dispersed,
Sunk, ravaged, ruined as my life
Has been, and will continue so
Until your death, since everything
Must serve again. Perhaps for us
Nothing can any more be new. Perhaps
Creation ceases or has ceased,
As almost everyone I know believes.
—And yet, at noon, I thought I saw
Two suns appear; deep in the forest
Where the stones sweat, where the new graves
Take the grass, a strange bird
Sang, who only sang at night before,
Sang in this doubled glare. I go on
Piling up the rubble and the stones
To build a kind of monument, for rest
Becomes insufferable. My hair
Is white as morning now; I doubt

That you would know me as I am.
I wonder sometimes if I would begin
This life of mine again, for I have mortified
My flesh and suffered punishment
Past all believing. That your own life
Should be happy is my deepest wish.
The light dies on the sill. The ordinary sun
Sinks on our wilderness. Until
Another time . . .

(THE CHILD CRUMPLES THE LETTER INTO A BALL
   AND TOSSES IT BACK INTO THE DEBRIS.)

THE BEACH IN AUGUST

The day the fat woman
In the bright blue bathing suit
Walked into the water and died,
I thought about the human
Condition. Pieces of old fruit
Came in and were left by the tide.

What I thought about the human
Condition was this: old fruit
Comes in and is left, and dries
In the sun. Another fat woman
In a dull green bathing suit
Dives into the water and dies.
The pulmotors glisten. It is noon.

We dry and die in the sun
While the seascape arranges old fruit,
Coming in with the tide, glistening
At noon. A woman, moderately stout,
In a nondescript bathing suit,
Swims to a pier. A tall woman
Steps toward the sea. One thinks about the human
Condition. The tide goes in and goes out.

ROBINSON AT HOME

Curtains drawn back, the door ajar.
All winter long, it seemed, a darkening
Began. But now the moonlight and the odors of the street
Conspire and combine toward one community.

These are the rooms of Robinson.
Bleached, wan, and colorless this light, as though
All the blurred daybreaks of the spring
Found an asylum here, perhaps for Robinson alone,

Who sleeps. Were there more music sifted through the floors
And moonlight of a different kind,
He might awake to hear the news at ten,
Which will be shocking, moderately.

This sleep is from exhaustion, but his old desire
To die like this has known a lessening.
Now there is only this coldness that he has to wear.
But not in sleep.—Observant scholar, traveller,

Or uncouth bearded figure squatting in a cave,
A keen-eyed sniper on the barricades,
A heretic in catacombs, a famed roué,
A beggar on the streets, the confidant of Popes—

All these are Robinson in sleep, who mumbles as he turns,
"There is something in this madhouse that I symbolize—
This city—nightmare—black—"
                                    He wakes in sweat
To the terrible moonlight and what might be
Silence. It drones like wires far beyond the roofs,
And the long curtains blow into the room.

136

A DISTANCE FROM THE SEA

To Ernest Brace

"And when the seven thunders had uttered their voices, I was about to write: and I heard a voice from heaven saying unto me, Seal up those things which the seven thunders uttered, and write them not." —REVELATIONS, X, 4.

That raft we rigged up, under the water,
Was just the item: when he walked,
With his robes blowing, dark against the sky,
It was as though the unsubstantial waves held up
His slender and inviolate feet. The gulls flew over,
Dropping, crying alone; thin ragged lengths of cloud
Drifted in bars across the sun. There on the shore
The crowd's response was instantaneous. He
Handled it well, I thought—the gait, the tilt of the head, just
   right.
Long streaks of light were blinding on the waves.
And then we knew our work well worth the time:
The days of sawing, fitting, all those nails,
The tiresome rehearsals, considerations of execution.
But if you want a miracle, you have to work for it,
Lay your plans carefully and keep one jump
Ahead of the crowd. To report a miracle
Is a pleasure unalloyed; but staging one requires
Tact, imagination, a special knack for the job
Not everyone possesses. A miracle, in fact, *means* work.
—And now there are those who have come saying
That miracles were not what we were after. But what else
Is there? What other hope does life hold out

But the miraculous, the skilled and patient
Execution, the teamwork, all the pain and worry every miracle
　　involves?

Visionaries tossing in their beds, haunted and racked
By questions of Messiahship and eschatology,
Are like the mist rising at nightfall, and come,
Perhaps, to even less. Grave supernaturalists, devoted wor-
　　shippers
Experience the ecstasy (such as it is), but not
Our ecstasy. It was our making. Yet sometimes
When the torrent of that time
Comes pouring back, I wonder at our courage
And our enterprise. It was as though the world
Had been one darkening, abandoned hall
Where rows of unlit candles stood; and we
Not out of love, so much, or hope, or even worship, but
Out of the fear of death, came with our lights
And watched the candles, one by one, take fire, flames
Against the long night of our fear. We thought
That we could never die. Now I am less convinced.
—The traveller on the plain makes out the mountains
At a distance; then he loses sight. His way
Winds through the valleys; then, at a sudden turning of a
　　path,
The peaks stand nakedly before him: they are something else
Than what he saw below. I think now of the raft
(For me, somehow, the summit of the whole experience)
And all the expectations of that day, but also of the cave
We stocked with bread, the secret meetings
In the hills, the fake assassins hired for the last pursuit,

138

The careful staging of the cures, the bribed officials,
The angels' garments, tailored faultlessly,
The medicines administered behind the stone,
That ultimate cloud, so perfect, and so opportune.
Who managed all that blood I never knew.

The days get longer. It was a long time ago.
And I have come to that point in the turning of the path
Where peaks are infinite—horn-shaped and scaly, choked with
    thorns.
But even here, I know our work was worth the cost.
What we have brought to pass, no one can take away.
Life offers up no miracles, unfortunately, and needs assistance.
Nothing will be the same as once it was,
I tell myself.—It's dark here on the peak, and keeps on getting
    darker.
It seems I am experiencing a kind of ecstasy.
Was it sunlight on the waves that day? The night comes down.
And now the water seems remote, unreal, and perhaps it is.

A SALVO FOR HANS HOFMANN

Out of the summer's heat, the winter's cold,
The look of harbors and the trees,

The slashed world traced and traced again,
Enriched, enlarged, caught in a burning scrutiny

Like fog-lamps on a rotten night. The scraps
Of living shift and change. Because of you,

The light burns sharper in how many rooms,
Shaped to a new identity; the dark hall

Finds a door; the wind comes in;
A rainbow sleeps and wakes against the wall.

Part Three

THE DARKNESS

I have seen it in the green tree
For a long time now,
In the shapes on pavements, oiled

And streaked with rain, and where
Hands have touched at doors.
Over the roofs and streets,

On face after passing face
I have watched it spread,
At the edge of the sky at noon

Until it stains the dead
Weeds in some empty place
And saturates the sun

—As though one had pulled a string
In an unfamiliar house,
Of a dim light, darkening.

THE COMING OF THE PLAGUE

September was when it began.
Locusts dying in the fields; our dogs
Silent, moving like shadows on a wall;
And strange worms crawling; flies of a kind
We had never seen before; huge vineyard moths;
Badgers and snakes, abandoning
Their holes in the field; the fruit gone rotten;
Queer fungi sprouting; the fields and woods
Covered with spiderwebs; black vapors
Rising from the earth—all these,
And more, began that fall. Ravens flew round
The hospital in pairs. Where there was water,
We could hear the sound of beating clothes
All through the night. We could not count
All the miscarriages, the quarrels, the jealousies.
And one day in a field I saw
A swarm of frogs, swollen and hideous,
Hundreds upon hundreds, sitting on each other,
Huddled together, silent, ominous,
And heard the sound of rushing wind.

THE FURIES

Not a third that walks beside me,
But five or six or more.
Whether at dusk or daybreak
Or at blinding noon, a retinue
Of shadows that no door
Excludes.—One like a kind of scrawl,
Hands scrawled trembling and blue,
A harelipped and hunchbacked dwarf
With a smile like a grapefruit rind,
Who jabbers the way I do
When the brain is empty and tired
And the guests no longer care:
A clown, who shudders and suddenly
Is a man with a mouth of cotton
Trapped in a dentist's chair.

Not a third that walks beside me,
But five or six or more:
One with his face gone rotten,
Most hideous of all,
Whose crutches shriek on the sidewalk
As a fingernail on a slate
Tears open some splintered door
Of childhood. Down the hall
We enter a thousand rooms
That pour the hours back,
That silhouette the walls
With shadows ripped from war,
Accusing and rigid, black

As the streets we are discolored by.
The crutches fall to the floor.

Not a third that walks beside me,
But five or six, or more
Than fingers or brain can bear—
A monster strung with guts,
A coward covered with hair,
Matted and down to his knees,
Murderers, liars, thieves,
Moving in darkened rows
Through daylight and evening air
Until the eyelids close,
Snapped like the blades of a knife,
And your dream of their death begins.
Possessors and possessed,
They keep the bedside wake
As a doctor or a wife
Might wait the darkness through
Until the pale daybreak—
Protectors of your life.

WET THURSDAY

To Lindley Williams Hubbell

A stiff wind off the channel
Linking the chimney's mutterings
With rain; the shaken trees,
Mile after mile, greening the sand.
Turn to the fire as the afternoon
Turns gray. Then suddenly
The locked door opens without a sound,
Thunder shaking the sky, to usher in
A monstrous cat that seems
Far older than the oldest carp
In the waters under the earth,
Moving like a shadow over the floor
To warm its frozen paws
Before the fire. He turns,
Smiling into the woodbox,
And says, *"Felis libyca domestica*
They call me, kept by man for catching
Rats and mice. Of Eastern or
Egyptian origin. Now to be
Your spiteful and envenomed shadow. Here
Will I live out my nine and evil lives
Before your very interesting fire.
And the days, months, years, are endless."

Wind pounds along the coast.
The trees bend double to the sand.
The cat sleeps like an old campaigner
During this season of the long rains.

145

EQUINOX

Under black lace the bald skull shines and nods,
A melon seasoned in this winter sun,
Bare, yellowed, finial
Above the claw-and-ball-foot chair that mourns
North toward the frozen window and the bay. The gulls
Rise in a long line off the rocks, steer
For the lighthouse, shadowing the boats
That toss, abandoned, far beyond the point.
Dead fish are heaped upon the coast for miles.
Her life is sleep, and pain. With wakening
To this sequestered and snow-haunted world,
The black mantilla creaks with frost; red eyes
Break through the rinds of flesh, blur
Toward the dripping faucet and the last cans of
Spaghetti and baked beans, corroding on the shelves.

A bubble, then a sound that borders on a word
Breaks from her mouth. If she could think,
Her eighty years would bend toward Spain—
Shadows of *santos,* crowds swarming in the heat,
Plumes, awnings, shields, the sun six hours high . ..

She believes this coast is in the South. A month ago,
Smoke from the village chimneys died. No lights burn
In windows of the cottages. Over the vacant docks
The birds are featureless, but her sight fails
Where these walls end.
                              Exile without remembrance,
Spawned in the heat to perish in this cold,
Ravaged by paresis, and her sight at last

A blackness in the blood, she moves her chair
Inch by excruciating inch, her face
Steered—raw, blank, aching—toward the beans:
The last survivor of the race.

RELATING TO ROBINSON

Somewhere in Chelsea, early summer;
And, walking in the twilight toward the docks,
I thought I made out Robinson ahead of me.

From an uncurtained second-story room, a radio
Was playing *There's a Small Hotel*; a kite
Twisted above dark rooftops and slow drifting birds.
We were alone there, he and I,
Inhabiting the empty street.

Under a sign for Natural Bloom Cigars,
While lights clicked softly in the dusk from red to green,
He stopped and gazed into a window
Where a plaster Venus, modeling a truss,
Looked out at Eastbound traffic. (But Robinson,
I knew, was out of town: he summers at a place in Maine,
Sometimes on Fire Island, sometimes the Cape,
Leaves town in June and comes back after Labor Lay.)
And yet, I almost called out, "Robinson!"

There was no chance. Just as I passed,
Turning my head to search his face,
His own head turned with mine
And fixed me with dilated, terrifying eyes
That stopped my blood. His voice
Came at me like an echo in the dark.

"I thought I saw the whirlpool opening.
Kicked all night at a bolted door.
You must have followed me from Astor Place.
An empty paper floats down at the last.

And then a day as huge as yesterday in pairs
Unrolled its horror on my face
Until it blocked—" Running in sweat
To reach the docks, I turned back
For a second glance. I had no certainty,
There in the dark, that it was Robinson
Or someone else.

                The block was bare. The Venus,
Bathed in blue fluorescent light,
Stared toward the river. As I hurried West,
The lights across the bay were coming on.
The boats moved silently and the low whistles blew.

JANUARY

Morning: blue, cold, and still.
Eyes that have stared too long
Stare at the wedge of light
At the end of the frozen room
Where snow on a windowsill,
Packed and cold as a life,
Winters the sense of wrong
And emptiness and loss
That is my awakening.
A lifetime drains away
Down a path of frost;
My face in the looking-glass
Turns again from the light
Toward fragments of the past
That break with the end of sleep.
This wakening, this breath
No longer real, this deep
Darkness where we toss,
Cover a life at the last.
Sleep is too short a death.

FARRAGO

The housings fall so low they graze the ground
And hide our human legs. False legs hang down
Outside. Dance in a horse's hide for a punctured god.

We killed and roasted one. And now he haunts the air,
Invisible, creates our world again, lights the bright star
And hurls the thunderbolt. His body and his blood

Hurry the harvest. Through the tall grain,
Toward nightfall, these cold tears of his come down like rain,
Spotting and darkening.—I sit in a bar

On Tenth Street, writing down these lies
In the worst winter of my life. A damp snow
Falls against the pane. When everything dies,

The days all end alike, the sound
Of breaking goes on faintly all around,
Outside and inside. Where I go,

The housings fall so low they graze the ground
And hide our human legs. False legs fall down
Outside. Dance in a horse's hide. Dance in the snow.

THE BASE

Poison is in the wood. The sap
Runs thin, the bark sheds off. We scaled
The tallest pine and found it rotting at the top.

And yet the lower leaves are green,
Or almost green, and scarcely thinning
Where the light is kind. Who sealed

Those veins and faked that color could
Shrivel the world's enormous skin
And make it burn and glow

Like all the lights of Europe. So
It burns and burns. The sap runs thin.
And here we build, and gather, and are fed.

COLLOQUY

In the broken light, in owl weather,
Webs on the lawn where the leaves end,
I took the thin moon and the sky for cover
To pick the cat's brains and descend
A weedy hill. I found him groveling
Inside the summerhouse, a shadowed bulge,
Furred and somnolent.—"I bring,"
I said, "besides this dish of liver, and an edge
Of cheese, the customary torments,
And the usual wonder why we live
At all, and why the world thins out and perishes
As it has done for me, sieved
As I am toward silences. Where
Are we now? Do we know anything?"
—Now, on another night, his look endures.
"Give me the dish," he said.
I had his answer, wise as yours.

THE UMBRELLA

To Conrad Aiken

Because, in the hot countries,
They worshipped trees; because,
Under the sacred figs, Gautama
Became a god; because of the rain,
Because the sun beats down.
Because we followed orders, building a tent
"Of ten curtains of fine twined linen,
And blue and purple and scarlet." And because
The ark required protection, with four pillars
Holding the curtains up, and "the veil
Shall divide unto you between the holy place
And the most holy."—I planted the seed
Of an elm and watered it. Rest
In the shelter of this shade. Black spines
Of metal and a tent of cloth
Are blooming where a tree stood up.

Discs float above the heads
Of the images
Of Indian gods. Sometimes
There are three of them, and each
Smaller than the one
That goes beneath. And sometimes
These tiers of aureoles
Are gone: umbrellas
Crown them in their place.

Two thousand years before the birth of Christ,
If there is any believing Chinese legend,

The wife of a carpenter named Lou Pan
Said to her husband one morning: "You and your father
Before you have built well My Lord. But your houses
Are rigid, immovable. Now that the grass
Goes brown with autumn, I will build roofs
One can carry about. I will build a pagoda
On a stick, to give shelter wherever one goes."
And this she proceeded to do.
                                When the Son
Of Heaven strode to the hunt, twenty-four umbrellas
Went before him. The Mikado proceeded in similar fashion
Under a red silk sunshade: emblem of "absolute power."
Protectors of kings and princes, floating
Over triumphal processions and battlefields,
Moving like a sea of tossing waves.
And in India, in 1877, the Prince of Wales
(Later Edward VII) moved in stately procession
Mounted on an elephant,
A gold umbrella before him. The Greeks
Hinted at secret rites of the umbrella cult.
At the Scirophoria, a priestess and a priest
"Went from the Acropolis to a place called Scira
Walking under a great white baldachino."
And during the Thesmophoria, slaves
Carried parasols over the heads of the women
Who brought gifts to Persephone at the temple,
Desiring fertility.—And when we left the corpses
Out of doors, we put umbrellas over them,
Not to shield them from the sun, but rather
To protect the sunlight against pollution
By the dead. The Pope's was carried by a man in armor

On a white horse. The English and the French
Trimmed them with ruches, valances, pompons,
Tassels, fringes, frills of lace, glass beads,
Sequins, artificial flowers, ostrich feathers,
God knows what else.

Over the empty harbor, gray and motionless,
The clouds have been gathering all afternoon, and now
The sea is pitted with rain. Wind shakes the house.
Here from this window lashed with spray, I watch
A black umbrella, ripped apart and wrong side out,
Go lurching wildly down the beach; a sudden gust
Carries it upward, upside down,
Over the water, flapping and free,
Into the heart of the storm.

SMALL PRAYER

Change, move, dead clock, that this fresh day
May break with dazzling light to these sick eyes.
Burn, glare, old sun, so long unseen,
That time may find its sound again, and cleanse
What ever it is that a wound remembers
After the healing ends.

UNCOLLECTED POEMS

TO BUILD A QUIET CITY IN HIS MIND

To build a quiet city in his mind:
A single overwhelming wish; to build,
Not hastily, for there is so much wind,
So many eager smilers to be killed,
Obstructions one might overlook in haste:
The ruined structures cluttering the past,

A little at a time and slow is best,
Crawling as though through endless corridors,
Remembering always there are many doors
That open to admit the captured guest
Once only.
              Yet in spite of loss and guilt
And hurricanes of time, it might be built:

A refuge, permanent, with trees that shade
When all the other cities die and fade.

TO A NOISY CONTEMPORARY

Your ego's bad dream drums that vision
Encountered on page one, pages three to eighty-nine.
Count the wound-up places where we went aground.
As an entertainment, zero. Hero horror. Try the line

Of incestuous relations, hearty friendship, or the cult
Of the ectoplasmic navel and the ravishments of guilt.

Page two was delightful. And the margins were wide;
One was tempted by the imagery of bloody wrists,
Your hysterogetic spasms and italicized reproofs.
You may well supplant the tuba if the music lasts.

THE OLDER PROGRAMS THAT WE FALSIFIED

The older programs that we falsified,
Tired comrades, float above our heads
Like frightened birds and will not be ignored.
Observable but silent, they have cried
To some of us for years, while sleepless in our beds
We thought we heard the gavel's welcome rapping, floored
Opponents who had long been dead,
Who took to drink or drugs or politics,
Or merely died, or carved out new careers
In government or in the theatre.
Not all of us, indeed, are here tonight.
Some joined the enemy (forgive my smile), some dragged their
    fears
To psychoanalysts or into the dark,
Or shot themselves in bathrooms. Has it been ten years?
So long as that? Well, here we are again.

PLACE OF EXECUTION

1.

Where are the marvelous cities that our childhoods built for
us,
With houses unlike those that we have come to know,
And the cathedrals and the violet streets? And all the rooms
Miraculously designed, warm as our nights, with friends at
every door?
Great towers, rich and yellowing, and churning seas
With cliffs to throw their breaking waves upon,
And immense suns, burning through the palms?

What happened to the predictions, all the promises
Of achievement, the golden beaches that we hurried to like
tides?
Where have the faces gone, the curtained windows
That opened on the park—green fields, green woods, green
distances,
The mirrored globes, returning our distorted smiles?

If we walk along the empty foreground of the sea,
The wind is cold, and there is only darkness at our backs.

2.

The world was a devious curvature, seen through the goldfish
bowl.
The fish swarm through a tidy universe of arching skies,
Weedstems, debris, white flakes of soggy nourishment,
And the moss on the castle waved languidly. But even then
The quarrels were constant. "Live my own life . . ."
Slamming of doors. "Night after night I've tried to sleep . . ."
And one day someone broke the goldfish bowl, or it fell;

Anyway, the fish were dead on the floor, among the broken
glass.
Everyone agreed it was fortunate that the cat had been out-
side.

3.
If you walk along the foreground of the sea
And watch the wheeling birds and the far boats,
Listening to the waves and the sound of oars—

What if there is no sea?
What if it roars a thousand miles from where you are?
What if the water flows down, down, down . . .

More probably you are conducting
An unwilled sociological investigation
Of a middle-class slum, or searching
At a doorway for the proper key,
Or staring from a window
(Streaked as though by tears)
At Christmas evergreens
That smoulder in an empty lot. The day
Is moving towards its unspectacular conclusion.
The streets are darkened and the lights come on.

We have arrived, finally, at the celebration
Where there is nothing to celebrate.
In a landscape of dubious interest
With odors of unaired rooms and the less pleasant aroma
Of last year's socio-economic predictions.
An erubescent Santa Claus grins from a window,
Sawdust running out of his side.

4.
The city wakens slowly in unmoving fog.
Pale colonnades and desecrated walls
Float and are gone beyond the *collage* of the roofs.
Below the rusty grillwork and the nailed-up doors,
Thin mournful cats prowl through the dirty snow.
The day takes on the color of the street.

What we have come to know
Are these emerging, undesired views,
These vacant and relentless dawns
That lengthen toward another afternoon.
What we have come to know
Are false predictions, shattered promises,
Our weakness and the loss of hope,
The loss of courage where both time
And celebration end.

The bowl breaks and the fish gasp on the floor.

The window offers graying colonnades,
Gray rooms where goldfish sample death again and flowers
    wilt.
Our eyes are strangers' eyes that haunt our childhood. There,
In distances of waste, the cities are unbuilt.

THAT FIGURE WITH THE MOULTING BEARD

That figure with the moulting beard and ancient stare
You thought you had escaped in Brooklyn Heights
You'll reckon with again, pursuing you down 63rd Street,
Yet quite unhurried, almost sanguine, one might say.
That time you'll lose him in the crowd, forget him until years
Have passed.—Then, two years later, in a suburb of Los
    Angeles,
On some dull rainy afternoon, you'll see his eyes,
Before a pawnshop strung with dusty mandolins
And open knives, stare from the same accusing face.
Again there will be time to leave, and no pursuit.

The last time will be years from now, and in the dark:
Here perhaps, perhaps in Wichita, perhaps along deserted
    roads.
But of the lead pipe in his pocket and the knife,
The torch, the poison, and the nails, no doubt at all.

THE BUNYIP

Feathered and gray, about the size
Of a full-grown calf, its long neck
Budded with an emu's head, covered

With fur. The voice (reportedly) is like
A thousand booming drums. It puzzled aborigines
Long before the white man came.

It lives in the sea. Its names
Are musical: Tumbata, Bunyip,
Kanjaprati, Melagi. From its back

A plume of water spouts, the terror of
The womenfolk of fishermen.
It crosses oceans into inland waters,

Crying sometimes, after dark, that it is not
Extinct, imaginary, or a myth—
Its feathers ruffled, and its voice

Not like a thousand drums at all,
But muffled, dwindling, hard to hear these nights
Like far-off foghorns that the wind throws back.

FIRST ANNIVERSARY

After you died, strangers from town
Wheeled the black wood you wore
To the big window. It was then
The walls, the ceiling, and the floor
Enlarged. The room was monstrous, overgrown.

Through that long afternoon, all we could share
Was space. All we have known
From that time on is fear. Again
The wheels turn and the silk-lined box is gone.
The room is dwarfed, immutable, and bare.

COVERING TWO YEARS

This nothingness that feeds upon itself:
Pencils that turn to water in the hand,
Parts of a sentence, hanging in the air,
Thoughts breaking in the mind like glass,
Blank sheets of paper that reflect the world
Whitened the world that I was silenced by.

There were two years of that. Slowly,
Whatever splits, dissevers, cuts, cracks, ravels, or divides
To bring me to that diet of corrosion, burned
And flickered to its terminal.—Now in an older hand
I write my name. Now with a voice grown unfamiliar,
I speak to silences of altered rooms,
Shaken by knowledge of recurrence and return.

A NAMELESS PLACE

Under what trees rehearse this catalog again?
A thunder of bees, clamorous with alarm,
Augments the welcome of the park. From narrow paths
The pram wheels streak the gravel, an old dog
Acquaints the lilac bushes, near the iron fence, with his scent.
A Sunday afternoon like any afternoon.

So there would be (and are) white blasts of steam
That rise now from the island's tallest old hotel,
That drift above the water tower's green,
The trees, brown roofs, the shingles drained of shade.

Beneath such colors, all the torments of your room,
Which loomed so elephantine and permanent,
Go into nothing northward like the steam,
And have become the torments of interiors—
Creatures that leap from walls, that hide
In wait behind the bedroom door, in packages,
And on hot pillows keep our cold thoughts company.

A Sunday afternoon like any afternoon.
The brooding heat of vegetation, profligate,
Swells from the broken fountain where
A gathering begins. Colleagues of those you left behind,
Intent, depraved, indomitable. From all the blue,
The bees' dull roar is loud with danger, and the park's
Iron fence shrinks toward you as the shriveling world
Moved inward years ago. Like any afternoon.
An afternoon like any afternoon.

THE EXPOSED REEF

Domed roof, gun-metal astragals
Light over broken water and dense spray
Above the cast-iron pedestal . . .

Tossed in the soaking kelp, I smash
My face against the lighthouse base
And watch, far out, the splintered boat

That rides toward land drifting like waste.
Light over broken water and dense spray
Breaks on the blood I might have coughed,

Or leaked in tropics, mailed in packages
To wounds that Europe still designs so perfectly.
But then I would not hear this singing blood,

Would not have learned, above the onslaught of the waves.
The domed roof and gun-metal astragals,
How the blood roars, "Man lives to drown

"Below this cast-iron pedestal
While the cold white warning light burns on."
I hear the boat smash on the rocks. The gulls

Scream through the darkness and the blinding spray.
As seamarks we preserve ourselves. After the storm,
The long line of the water, churned toward Marathon.

RITES FOR WINTER

Now, to those dawns swept up from poles
In the long rush of February storms
—When flakes are swept through darkness to the north
And mountains of blue ice are metal to the sun—
Offer no light, no fire. Your nakedness,
The numbed and empty hand, is perfect offering,
The blood unthawed, the small bones of the frost.

Without this ritual, among these plains of ice,
The black snows of the later year are stayed—
Black snows that rage before the warmth returns,
Turning to rains, slow rains that end
As suns roll thunder through divisioned skies.
Exposure moves the blood again, the veins are warm,
Green worlds rehearse to winter eyes.

IF THIS ROOM IS OUR WORLD

If this room is our world, then let
This world be damned. Open this roof
For one last monstrous flood
To sweep away this floor, these chairs,
This bed that takes me to no sleep.
Under the black sky of our circumstance,
Mumbling of wet barometers, I stare
At cities dust that soils the glass
While thunder perishes. The heroes perish
Miles from here. Their blood runs heavy in the grass,
Sweet, restless, clotted, sickening,
Runs to the rivers and the seas, the seas
That are the source of that devouring flood
That I await, that I must perish by.

THE END OF THE LIBRARY

When the coal
Gave out, we began
Burning the books, one by one;
First the set
Of Bulwer-Lytton
And then the Walter Scott.
They gave a lot of warmth.
Toward the end, in
February, flames
Consumed the Greek
Tragedians and Baudelaire,
Proust, Robert Burton
And the Po-Chu-i. Ice
Thickened on the sills.
More for the sake of the cat,
We said, than for ourselves,
Who huddled, shivering,
Against the stove
All winter long.

LATE EVENING SONG

For a while
Let it be enough:
The responsive smile,
Though effort goes into it.

Across the warm room
Shared in candlelight,
This look beyond shame,
Possible now, at night,

Goes out to yours.
Hidden by day
And shaped by fires
Grown dead, gone gray,

That burned in other rooms I knew
Too long ago to mark,
It forms again. I look at you
Across those fires and the dark.

A MUSICIAN'S WIFE

Between the visits to the shock ward
The doctors used to let you play
On the old upright Baldwin
Donated by a former patient
Who is said to be quite stable now.

And all day long you played Chopin,
Badly and hauntingly, when you weren't
Screaming on the porch that looked
Like an enormous birdcage. Or sat
In your room and stared out at the sky.

You never looked at me at all.
I used to walk down to where the bus stopped
Over the hill where the eucalyptus trees
Moved in the fog, and stared down
At the lights coming on, in the white rooms.

And always, when I came back to my sister's
I used to get out the records you made
The year before all your terrible trouble,
The records the critics praised and nobody bought
That are almost worn out now.

Now, sometimes I wake in the night
And hear the sound of dead leaves
Against the shutters. And then a distant
Music starts, a music out of an abyss,
And it is dawn before I sleep again.

THE CATS

What the cats do
To amuse themselves
When we are gone
I do not know.
They have the yard
And the fences
Of the neighbors,
And, occasionally,
May arrive at the door, miaowing,
With drops of milk
On their chins,
Waving their shining tails
And exhibiting signs of alarm
When the light inside
The refrigerator
Goes on. But what
They do all day
Remains a mystery.
It is a dull neighborhood.
Children scream
From the playground.
The cars go by in a bluish light.
At six o'clock the cats run out
When we come home from work
To greet us, crying, dancing,
After the long day.

ACKNOWLEDGMENTS

THE LAST MAN was Number Three of the Poetry Booklets from the Colt Press (San Francisco: 1943). Some of these poems first appeared in *Poetry* (Chicago), *The Kenyon Review, New Directions, Compass, Signatures, Partisan Review, New Poems: 1940, Vice Versa, Diogenes, Providence Journal.*

THE FALL OF THE MAGICIANS was published by Reynal & Hitchcock (New York: 1947). Some of these poems first appeared in *Accent, The American Mercury, Chimera, Common Sense, Diogenes, Furioso, Harper's Bazaar, Kenyon Review, The Nation, New Directions, The New Yorker, Partisan Review, Poetry Quarterly* (London), *Poetry: A Magazine of Verse, Politics, Portfolio, The Sewanee Review, Sundial, Vice Versa.*

POEMS 1947–1954 was published by Adrian Wilson (San Francisco: 1954). Most of these poems were first published in the following magazines: *Partisan Review, The New Yorker, Furioso, Botteghe Oscure, Poetry: A Magazine of Verse, The New Republic, Harper's Magazine, Perspective,* and *The Tiger's Eye;* and I am grateful to their editors for permission to include them here. The following poems appeared originally in *The New Yorker:* "Robinson at Home," "Aspects of Robinson," "Wet Thursday," and "Colloquy." "A Pastiche for Eve" accompanied the reproduction of a painting by Robert Motherwell in the portfolio *Women,* edited by Samuel M. Kootz, which appeared in 1947. "A Salvo for Hans

179

Hofmann" appeared in the catalog of a retrospective show of Hofmann's work in Paris in 1949. I want to acknowledge a particular debt to Mr. Norris Getty for his suggestions and continual helpfulness over a long period of years.—W.K.

UNCOLLECTED POEMS first appeared in the Stone Wall Press edition of *The Collected Poems of Weldon Kees* (Iowa City: 1960). Several of these poems were first published in *Furioso, Poetry: A Magazine of Verse, Prairie Schooner,* and *The New Republic.* "First Anniversary" was first published in *Perspective* (Spring 1954), and has not previously been collected.